D1062789

THIS BOOK IS PRESENTED TO:

....

ON THIS DAY:

....

OTHER BOOKS BY MARK BATTERSON

FOR KIDS

The Circle Maker for Kids (picture book)

FOR TEENS

The Circle Maker Student Edition

All In Student Edition

Praying Circles Around Your Future

FOR ADULTS

The Circle Maker

All In

Draw the Circle

Praying Circles Around the Lives of Your Children

The Circle Maker

DEVOTIONS FOR KIDS

Mark Batterson

ZONDERKIDZ

The Circle Maker Devotions for Kids
Copyright © 2018 by Mark Batterson

This title is also available as a Zondervan ebook.

Requests for information should be addressed to:
Zonderkidz, *3900 Sparks Dr. SE, Grand Rapids, Michigan 49546*

ISBN 978-0-310-76681-0

All Scripture quotations, unless otherwise indicated, are taken from The
Holy Bible, New International Version®, NIV®. Copyright © 1973, 1978, 1984,
2011 by Biblica, Inc.® Used by permission of Zondervan. All rights reserved
worldwide. www.Zondervan.com. The "NIV" and "New International
Version" are trademarks registered in the United States Patent and
Trademark Office by Biblica, Inc.®

Any Internet addresses (websites, blogs, etc.) and telephone numbers in this
book are offered as a resource. They are not intended in any way to be or
imply an endorsement by Zondervan, nor does Zondervan vouch for the
content of these sites and numbers for the life of this book.

All rights reserved. No part of this publication may be reproduced, stored in
a retrieval system, or transmitted in any form or by any means—electronic,
mechanical, photocopy, recording, or any other—except for brief quotations
in printed reviews, without the prior permission of the publisher.

Author is represented by the literary agency of The Fedd Agency, Inc., P.O.
Box 341973, Austin, Texas, 78734.

Zonderkidz is a trademark of Zondervan.

Interior design: Denise Froehlich

Printed in China

18 19 20 21 22 / DSC / 10 9 8 7 6 5 4 3 2 1

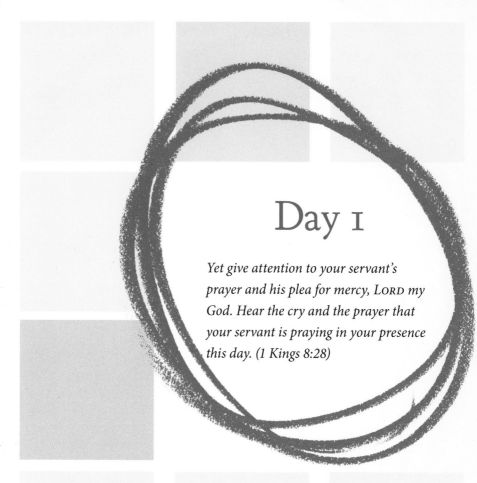

Day 1

Yet give attention to your servant's prayer and his plea for mercy, LORD my God. Hear the cry and the prayer that your servant is praying in your presence this day. (1 Kings 8:28)

The legend of Honi the circle maker shows how prayer can change the course of history. As Israel suffered a dreadful first-century drought, Honi made a bold step of faith. He called out to the Lord in prayer by drawing a circle in the sand and declaring that he wouldn't step out of it until it rained.

The Lord answered by opening the sky. Each raindrop served as a reminder of God's grace. It refreshed the dry ground, and it refreshed the faith of all the people watching. "Not for such rain have I prayed," Honi said from the circle, "but for rain of your favor, blessing, and graciousness."

Like Noah, who kept building an ark day after day (Genesis

6:9–22), we hammer away at the dream God has given us. Like the Israelites, who kept circling Jericho for seven days, we circle God's promises (Joshua 6). Like Elijah, who kept sending his servant to look for a rain cloud, we actively and expectantly wait for God's answer (1 Kings 18:43).

The earth has circled the sun more than two thousand times since the day Honi drew his circle in the sand, but God is still looking for circle makers. The timeless truth of this ancient legend is that bold prayers honor God, and God honors bold prayers.

Lord, I pray that you listen. I understand things won't always happen the way I expect, but I know you answer in your wisdom and timing. Start with my heart. Change me from the inside out.

Prayers I'm Circling

....

....

....

....

....

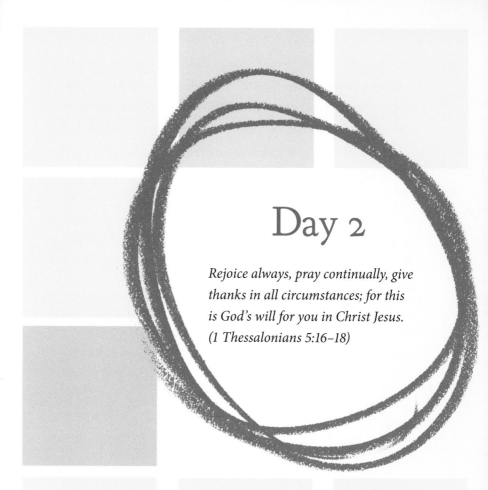

Day 2

Rejoice always, pray continually, give thanks in all circumstances; for this is God's will for you in Christ Jesus. (1 Thessalonians 5:16–18)

The story of the circle maker offers a new image of prayer. If praying was like coloring, we could scribble all over the place, scratching here and scratching there. Or we could draw circles. The circles could widen, like a target around a bull's-eye. Or the circles could be the same size but different shades of color around the same point. Just as a page of circles is more ordered than a page of scribbles, a prayer that circles has order too.

Making circles in prayer starts in the Bible. You can circle verses or promises on paper. And then you can "circle it" in prayer, meaning you pray about it and then circle back and pray about it more. Don't just pray a little and then move on to other things. This isn't one-and-done prayer. Praying a circle means returning to it again and again.

You can't *draw* a circle around a person or a classroom or a whole house, but you can still circle them with prayer. Shine a spotlight on a person you want to pray for, and then pray again and again for them. Think of lassoing a place like a super cowboy, and then pray specifically for it. The possibilities are as endless as a circle!

God, what verse should I circle in the Bible? What should I lasso in prayer?

Prayers I'm Circling

....

....

....

....

....

....

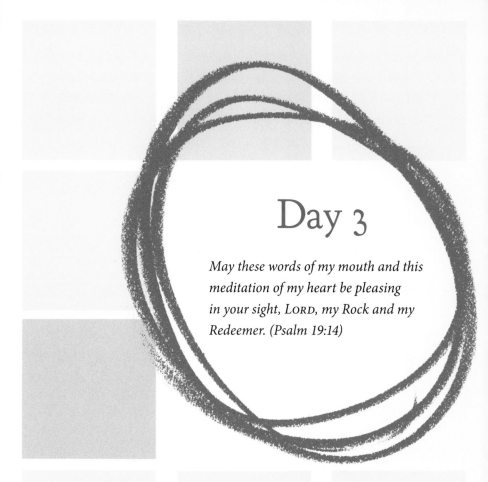

Day 3

May these words of my mouth and this meditation of my heart be pleasing in your sight, Lord, my Rock and my Redeemer. (Psalm 19:14)

Drawing prayer circles is a metaphor that simply means "praying until God answers." It's a decision to pray for as long as it takes, even if it takes longer than you ever imagined.

Drawing circles helps keep your focus, like an archer keeps their eye on the circle of a target. Sometimes drawing a circle of prayer might be around a promise or verse in the Bible. It may be around an idea or a dream. But you can draw *physical* circles of prayer too. A teacher might pray as she circles her classroom; a student might pray as he walks around his home; a team of doctors might turn their patient visits into prayer circles. Start praying, and God will help you zero in on a target.

There is nothing magical about physically circling something in prayer, but there is something biblical about it. The Israelites circled the city of Jericho until the wall came down. That's what daily prayer is all about. Too often we quit circling almost as soon as we start.

Drawing prayer circles isn't some magic trick to get what you want from God. God is not a genie in a bottle, and your wish is not his command. His command better be your wish. If it's not, you won't be drawing prayer circles; you'll end up walking in circles.

Lord, what do you want me to focus on? What do you want me to pray about and wait on? Help me walk through doors you open. Teach me to pray for as long as it takes.

Prayers I'm Circling

....

....

....

....

....

....

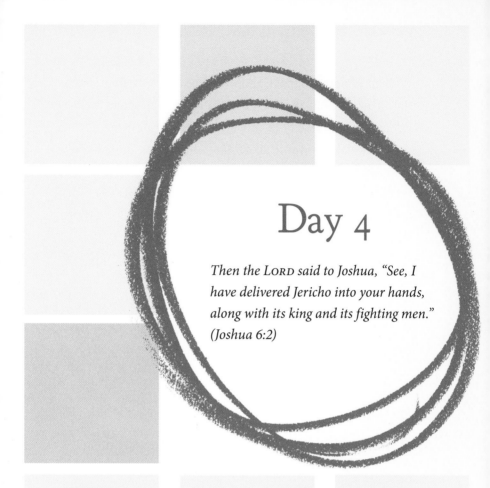

Day 4

Then the LORD said to Joshua, "See, I have delivered Jericho into your hands, along with its king and its fighting men." (Joshua 6:2)

The first glimpse of Jericho was both amazing and frightening. While wandering in the wilderness for forty years, the Israelites had never seen anything like the skyline of Jericho. The closer they got, the smaller they felt. They finally understood why their grandparents had felt too weak and small to enter the promised land.

Jericho was a guarded city, surrounded by walls as thick as a Volkswagen and as tall as three stacked double-decker buses. No one short of God Almighty could get past this fortress. God himself promised the impossible with a battle plan that made no sense to his people. March the entire army around the city once a day for six days, he said. On the seventh day, march around the city seven times.

Every soldier in the army must have wondered why. Why not use a battering ram? Why not scale the walls? Why not cut off the water supply or shoot flaming arrows over the walls? By the evening on the seventh day, they began their final lap. Then the priests sounded their horns and 600,000 Israelites raised a holy roar, and the walls of Jericho came tumbling down.

The image of the Israelites circling Jericho is a moving picture of what drawing prayer circles looks like. We face big obstacles and problems in our own lives, but they are no match for God. Take God at his word and prayerfully circle the amazing things he's said.

Thank you, God, that I can rely on your words, your power, and your wisdom. I praise you!

Prayers I'm Circling

....

....

....

....

....

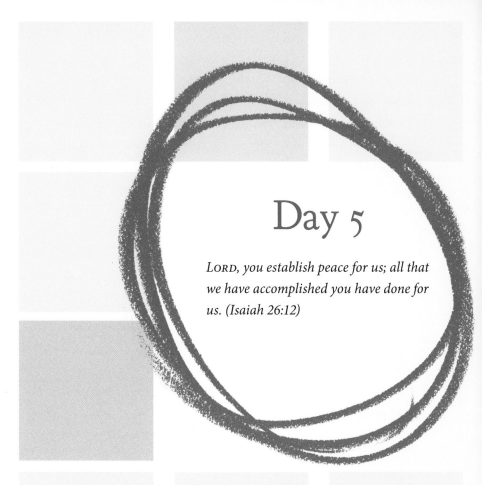

Day 5

LORD, you establish peace for us; all that we have accomplished you have done for us. (Isaiah 26:12)

Drawing prayer circles is a partnership with God. It's pushing open the door that he has already unlocked. It's making God's will into your will too. Getting what *you* want isn't the goal. The goal is to worship and spotlight God by drawing circles around the promises, miracles, and dreams *he* wants for you.

The opportunities for prayer are endless. You can draw prayer circles around promises in the Bible as well as promises the Holy Spirit puts on your heart. You can pray around difficult situations and goals. You can circle places and people.

Say you're having a hard time with someone at school. A girl looks at you and whispers to her friends, who laugh. She doesn't talk to you or smile, but she's definitely talking *about* you . . . in a bad way. It happens all the time, but the teacher never catches it, and your own friends don't get it. As a result, you feel especially alone. Except you aren't alone—God has your back and is waiting to be invited into your school and into your hurt. So you pray circles around the girl, her attitude, your wounds. You pray for wisdom for how to handle it the next time. You pray that the vibe in the entire classroom will change. You pray blessing on you and blessing on the girl. You pray dependence on God in the good and bad.

Praying circles might not be simple, easy, or quick, but you will be blessed to work through it with God. Because in prayer, we learn to rest in his presence. Raw dependence is the raw material out of which God performs his greatest miracles.

What do you want me to circle in prayer, Lord? What do you want to accomplish through me and in me?

Prayers I'm Circling

....

....

....

....

....

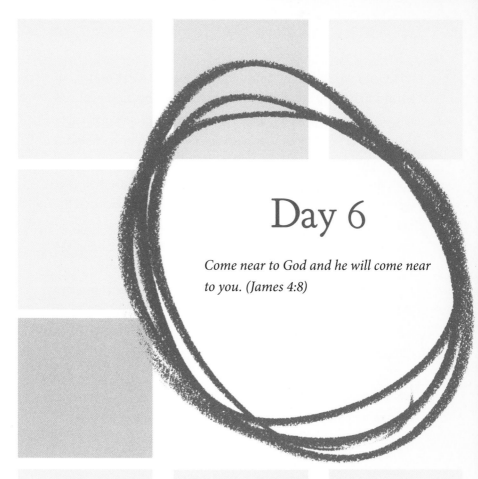

Day 6

Come near to God and he will come near to you. (James 4:8)

Prayer isn't listing our plans and wishes to God as a divine to-do list. The true purpose of prayer is to come before the Lord so he can share his will for us.

Here's your challenge: learn about prayer. Be a student when it comes to your personal relationship with God. If you like science, go about it scientifically: pray and observe, take notes, experiment. If you like art, go about it artistically: pray and be inspired, write poetry, or draw about what God shows you. Take pictures as inspiration for your prayer life. Keep a notebook, sketchbook, or journal that is personal to you and God. Don't forget to welcome him into your new process.

Along the way you will make new discoveries that will change the way you pray. And when you change the way you pray, life changes in exciting ways. Hope starts to fill your heart, and wisdom starts to fill your brain.

Talk to God about his Word (the Bible), the secrets of your heart, the details of your life. Share with him your problems and your victories. Have a tough teacher? Tell him about it. Got your best score on a spelling test? Tell him about it. And then listen. Be quiet so you can hear from the Lord himself. It might seem hard or weird at first, but you'll get used to listening. It will get easier and even exciting.

Teach me to pray, Lord. Teach me to listen.

Prayers I'm Circling

....

....

....

....

....

....

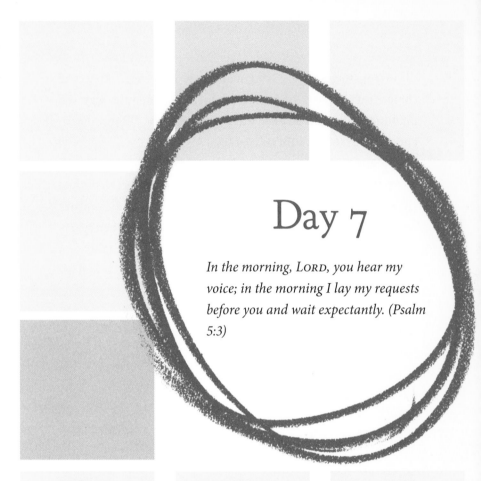

Day 7

In the morning, LORD, you hear my voice; in the morning I lay my requests before you and wait expectantly. (Psalm 5:3)

Prayer is not a one-and-done deal. It's not like a birthday party where you catch up with God once a year. It's more like an ordinary meal with the family that you do once a day (or more than once a day).

It's helpful to make a daily appointment with God by picking a time and place to pray. Maybe give God the first few minutes of the day. When you pray in the morning, it's like the whole day becomes a prayer. Get on your knees to remember you're God's servant. And when you do so, it's a reminder to see things from God's higher viewpoint and listen for his voice the rest of the day.

In our church, we circled 2 Chronicles 7:14 by getting on our knees every day at 7:14 a.m. The specific time isn't what matters. But the numbers on the clock offered a daily reminder of the promise we were circling in prayer: "If my people, who are called by my name, will humble themselves and pray and seek my face and turn from their wicked ways, then I will hear from heaven, and I will forgive their sin and will heal their land." On the first day of the prayer challenge, I dropped to my knees right after I got out of bed. This daily habit hasn't stopped yet.

Make prayer as regular as brushing your teeth. At first, you might need a cue to remember to pray. So put a reminder in place: set an alarm, tape a note to your door, put your prayer journal next to your bed. Once you create a routine, you will be ready to launch.

God, I'm excited about getting closer to you. I'm going to help myself remember, but remind me too, Lord.

Prayers I'm Circling

....

....

....

....

....

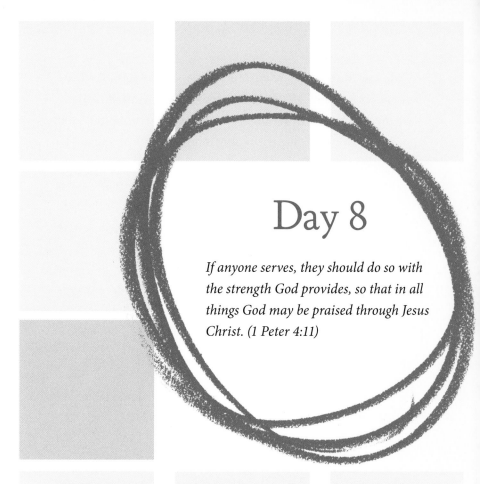

Day 8

If anyone serves, they should do so with the strength God provides, so that in all things God may be praised through Jesus Christ. (1 Peter 4:11)

Not long ago, a guy named Adam went on a mission trip to Ethiopia with our church. While he was there, he felt God calling him to give more than one week of his life. God's call became clearer when he saw a boy crawl out of a sewer manhole. This boy, named Lilly, was fifteen years old and without a home, without even sandals on his feet. Adam gave Lilly his own shoes, and Lilly gave Adam a tour of an entire community of orphans who lived under the streets. In that moment, Adam knew that Ethiopia—specifically the sewer—was his to circle in prayer.

Trusting God, Adam moved to Ethiopia. He started a ministry called Change Boys, which rescues street kids and gives them a home to live in. Without knowing exactly how God would provide, Adam signed a lease on a house in Ethiopia. He wasn't aware that his church family had been raising money to pay for the first year of the Ethiopian house. Now more than twenty orphans live with Adam in a house that God provided!

Should you think about moving to another country by yourself to start a new ministry? Maybe not. Even Jesus' ministry didn't start until he was a lot older. But just like Jesus when he was your age, you can learn God's Word and pray. Focus on your relationship with the heavenly Father, and who knows where he will tell you to go as you grow.

Lord, I trust you with the small details of my life right now, and I trust you with my future. Thank you for providing for me and covering me with your love.

Prayers I'm Circling

....

....

....

....

....

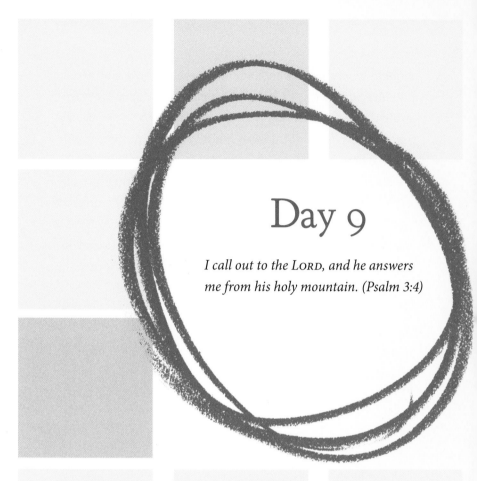

Day 9

I call out to the LORD, and he answers me from his holy mountain. (Psalm 3:4)

My grandfather had a prayer ritual that involved kneeling next to his bed at night, taking out his hearing aid, and praying for his family. He couldn't hear himself, but everyone else in the house could. It's pretty inspiring to hear someone pray for you by name. Grandpa died when I was six years old, but his prayers did not. At critical points in my life, the Spirit of God has whispered to me that the prayers of my grandfather were being answered in my life long after my grandfather had passed on.

You may never see how God answers your prayers. You might move away, go to a new school, or start attending a new church. As a result, you may be distant from all the things you've been praying for. But God is never distant from those things. He never forgets about them or gets sidetracked by other concerns. And he always answers prayer.

Think about this too: you might be witnessing answers to other people's prayer. Maybe Mom was praying about the new house, and nothing was lost in the move. Maybe your bro was praying circles around your new school, and you got the best teacher. Maybe Dad prayed to find a new church where the entire family could grow, learn, and enjoy.

The prayer offerings of someone else may be your praise offerings. So praise God for your new room or your new teacher or the new sermon about God's amazing love for you. Be grateful. Worship him. Pray and praise. You never know when your prayers will be answered, and you never know when you are the answer to someone else's prayer.

I praise you, Lord. Thank you for faithfully answering prayer.

Prayers I'm Circling

....

....

....

....

....

Day 10

For where two or three gather in my name, there am I with them. (Matthew 18:20)

Circling something in prayer means focusing on one thing, like a bull's-eye. Like the circles on the target, a person can pray around one thing many times. If you're concerned about moving to a new school, here are some circles you could pray. 1) Pray for yourself—that you move through your worry and stay positive, that you stay calm, that you keep smiling. 2) Pray for friends—that God moves another believer toward you, that you can find common ground with other students. 3) Pray for the teacher—that her classroom is filled with laughter and learning, that she sees God's grace in her day. 4) Pray for the school—that it stays safe, that God will be at work there. Those are four ideas to get you started, but you could keep circling with your specific fears, concerns, and praises.

Another way to circle is to invite people to pray with you. When two or three join you to pray together, they are forming a prayer circle around the dream or problem that you are circling. It's like super circling! Clue in your family about your prayers, and ask them to join you. Something great happens when we agree in prayer. That doesn't mean gathering some friends, walking to the store, holding hands, and bowing heads around your favorite bike. But if you are praying that God's will be done and to praise the Lord, then praying with someone is powerful.

Lord, thank you that you are in this place, present, and listening to my heart. I'm excited to pray with my family or my friends and see what you carry out.

Prayers I'm Circling

....

....

....

....

....

....

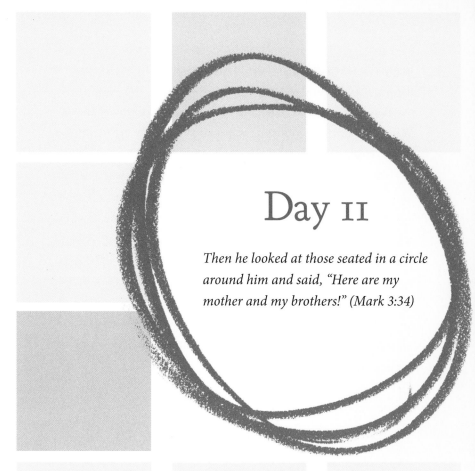

Day 11

Then he looked at those seated in a circle around him and said, "Here are my mother and my brothers!" (Mark 3:34)

Planets circle the sun like Christmas ornaments in space. The moon shines on earth from 238,885 miles away. The earth measures 24,900 miles around. God Almighty is above them all. Isaiah 40:22 says God sits on a throne above the circle of the earth. That is one big circle.

On a miniature scale, bubbles puff up to form 3-D circles called spheres. Flashlights shine circles on the wall. Wedding rings form unending lines of gold. People hold hands to form a circle of prayer. Honi drew a circle in the dirt.

If you hang out with a certain "circle of people," you share their interest or activity. If you "circle the wagons," you're uniting with others to defend against danger. To "come full circle" means to arrive back at the starting point. A circle is chain of events or parts that form a connected whole, so a circle suggests completion, safety, wholeness.

If you apply circles to prayer, you pray as continuously as a ring of gold. You pray not just once but until what you pray for is complete. You pray for things as big as the earth or as small as a bubble. You can pray with others in a prayer circle or pray full circle on your own.

Will your days be a three-ring circus or full of prayer circles? Invite the Lord in.

Lord, I see how I can picture a circle when I pray. I want to use that image to grow in prayer.

Prayers I'm Circling

....

....

....

....

....

....

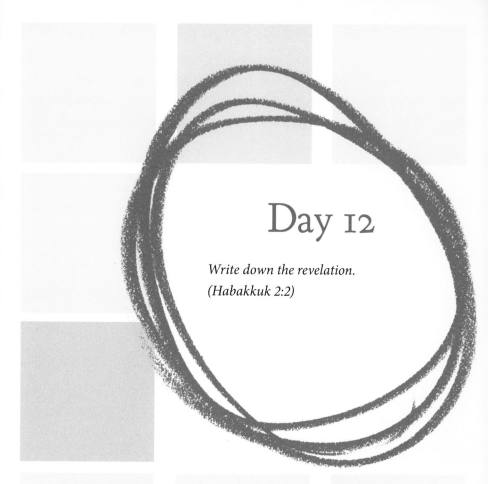

Day 12

Write down the revelation.
(Habakkuk 2:2)

Isn't it true that bad things seem easier to remember and blessings seem easier to forget? What if your brother rips your favorite T-shirt or your friend insults you in an argument? Do you hold on to a grudge or forgive and forget?

In the Bible, God told his people to build memorials so they would remember the good things, especially signs of his faithfulness. Instead of building a memorial, keep a journal to help you remember that you're a child of God. Fill a simple notebook with your personal requests of God, answers to prayer, lessons from church, important Bible verses, and daily gratitude. A journal is as individual and as special as you are.

You can keep your journal next to your bed to remind you to pray. Or you can take it wherever you go. At school, you might think of a prayer request you want to remember. At church, you might take notes so that you can pray about it later. If you see something on TV, you might write it down so you can process it later in prayer. Maybe keep your journal handy when you're praying. Keep a list of people to help you pray consistently and specifically. Maybe journal your thoughts on the Bible. Then, every once in a while, go back through it and circle the things you need to keep praying through.

Try journaling. See what works for you.

God, I'm excited to start journaling and to see where you take me.

Prayers I'm Circling

....

....

....

....

....

....

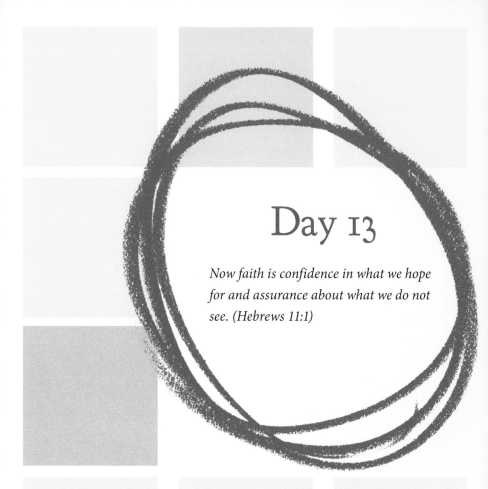

Day 13

Now faith is confidence in what we hope for and assurance about what we do not see. (Hebrews 11:1)

Circle makers are risk takers. God-follower Honi stepped into a circle in the dirt and promised to stay there until rain ended Israel's drought. He wasn't there alone—God was with him. Honi made a move in faith. God was going to make a move in a miracle. Honi didn't draw a semicircle; he drew a complete circle and then he prayed.

Drawing prayer circles around big things (even miracles) often looks kind of silly. Noah looked a little silly building a boat in the middle of a desert—before he was saved from the flood. The Israelite army looked silly marching around Jericho blowing trumpets—before the walls came tumbling down. David looked a little silly charging a giant with only a slingshot—before he killed Goliath. The Magi looked silly following a star—before they discovered the Messiah in a manger. Peter looked silly getting out of a boat in the middle of the Sea of Galilee—before he walked on water.

Each one of these Bible figures had a relationship with the God. They prayed. They listened. They followed. A relationship with the Lord paves the way for faith. Faith then paves the way for the miracle. So don't worry about looking silly. You're in good company.

Lord, I love you, and I want a close relationship with you. I want to grow faith. So, here I am, on my knees, listening to you in faith.

Prayers I'm Circling

....

....

....

....

....

....

Day 14

[He] prayed to God regularly. (Acts 10:2)

F ive words say everything you need to know about Cornelius, the Roman army officer mentioned in the verse above: he prayed to God regularly. The Bible doesn't record exactly when or where or how he prayed. It doesn't reveal whether he spoke to the Lord silently or out loud. It doesn't say if he prayed alone or with others. It doesn't tell us if he stood, sat, walked, kneeled, or laid down. Maybe he did a little bit of all of them. But this we know for sure: he prayed regularly.

One day Cornelius had a vision while praying in Caesarea. At the same time, the apostle Peter had a vision while praying in Joppa. As a result, Peter went to see Cornelius. Their meeting changed history! Until then, the gospel was reserved for the Jewish people. But when Cornelius put his faith in Jesus Christ, the door of salvation swung wide open to the Gentiles (non-Jews) too. The good news of the Son of God came into everyone's reach!

It all started with two people praying. Cornelius and Peter should have never met each other. Never. Ever. The average person in the first century didn't travel thirty miles away from home. And Roman soldiers and Jewish disciples didn't hang out. But when you pray to God regularly, irregular things happen on a regular basis. If we get on our knees, God will take us places we never imagined by paths we didn't even know existed.

Thank you, God, that your plans are made clear in your presence. I know that the same God who was with Peter and Cornelius is with me. Use me in your plans.

Prayers I'm Circling

....

....

....

....

....

....

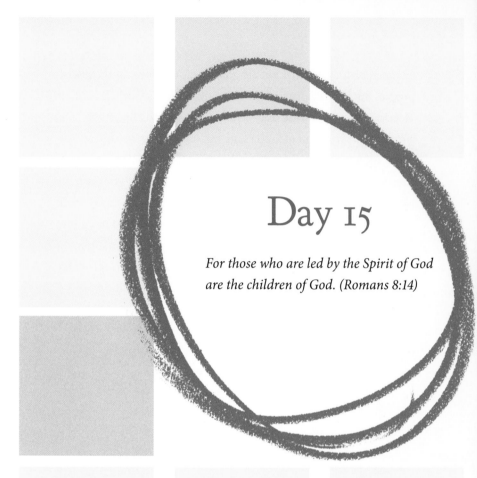

Day 15

For those who are led by the Spirit of God are the children of God. (Romans 8:14)

If you establish a prayer routine, your life will be anything but routine. Prayer brings you into the presence of an infinite, glorious God who has bigger plans for you than you imagine for yourself. The Spirit wants to reveal his hope, love, and glory to the world. And you, my friend, are invited on the adventure.

When you follow the leading of the Holy Spirit, you can't predict who you'll meet, where you'll go, or what you'll do. You don't need to make all kinds of grand plans. All you have to do is seek God in prayer.

Who you know—the heavenly Father—is far more important than what you know. You don't have to be an expert in

Hebrew to follow God day by day. You don't have to know the significance of the Dead Sea Scrolls to love your neighbor. You don't have to know the detailed history of ancient Israel to get on your knees. Don't try to make things happen. If you meet with God, God will make sure everything happens at the right time. Don't try to make your own miracles. Don't try to answer your own prayers. Don't try to do God's job for him. Stay humble. Stay patient. Stay focused. Keep praying.

You, Lord, are my leader. As I get in the habit of praying, I will keep my eyes on you. I want to listen to you and follow your voice and live your adventure.

Prayers I'm Circling

....

....

....

....

....

....

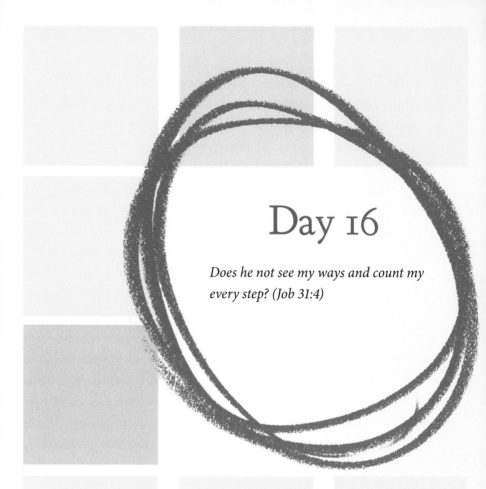

Day 16

Does he not see my ways and count my every step? (Job 31:4)

It may feel like you are sitting still right now, but you aren't. You are on a planet that is spinning at around 1,000 miles per hour. Every 24 hours, it circles the sun at nearly 67,000 miles per hour! Every day, you travel more than 1.5 million miles through space. When was the last time you prayed, "Lord, thanks for keeping the planet moving. I wasn't sure if we'd make the full rotation today, but you did it again!"?

We don't doubt God's ability to keep the planets in orbit, but we have a difficult time believing he can keep our lives on track. Which is more difficult—keeping the planets in order or determining our steps? We often trust God for big things. We need to also trust him for personal things, like getting through tough subjects at school, steering through trouble with friends, healing family illness. They are giant mountains to us, but prayer can turn them into molehills! God is great because nothing is too big for him, but also because nothing is too small.

The Lord cares about every detail of our lives. Every act of obedience, no matter how little, makes our heavenly Father proud. Every bit of faith—even a faith as small as a mustard seed—puts a smile on his face. Every sacrifice, no matter how insignificant it may seem to us, makes a difference. Just like your parents cheered when you took your first wobbly step, God rejoices over every baby step of faith. And he can turn those small steps into giant leaps.

Thank you, God, that you care about the world. And thank you that you care about me.

Prayers I'm Circling

....

....

....

....

....

....

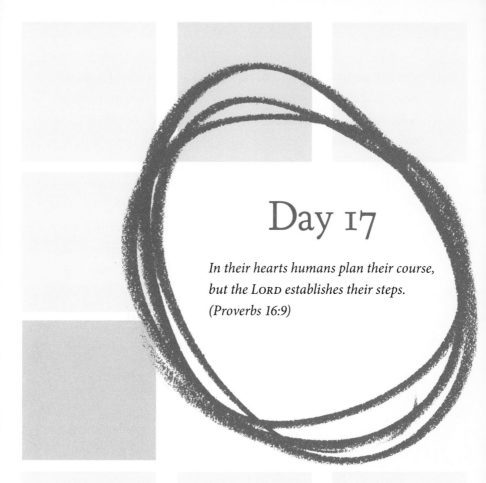

Day 17

*In their hearts humans plan their course,
but the LORD establishes their steps.
(Proverbs 16:9)*

God is with us. He cares for us, cares for where we are headed, and cares about the steps we take to get there.

In the above verse, write the Hebrew word *kûn* above the word *establishes*. *Kûn* is a word worth adding to your vocabulary. It's a careful word that reveals God makes plans right down to the smallest detail. It's a helpful word that celebrates God's ability to use everything for good. It's a calming word that suggests confidence in the fact that God has everything under control. It's a creative word that hints at the beauty of God's artistry.

God is the composer. Your life is his musical score. God is the artist. Your life is his canvas. God is the architect. Your life is his blueprint. God is the writer. You are his book. Each of these things goes hand in hand with the other, but they can't be swapped. Don't confuse our roles with God's. We can't perform miracles. All we can do is pray for them. Our job is to listen to God's voice. His job is to establish our steps.

If you're struggling to forgive your sister, pray, and go knock on her bedroom door. If you're wondering how to welcome the new kid at school, pray, and know that God will give you an opportunity. If you're hoping not to get caught for a bad decision, pray, and ask God what to do. He will direct your steps.

Utterly dependable, always faithful, the Lord makes even your steps secure (kûn). Rest and pray as you trust in him.

Thank you, Lord, for loving me, lighting my path, and directing my steps. It gives me confidence to trust in you. I want to watch you work, Lord. Open my eyes and use me.

Prayers I'm Circling

....

....

....

....

....

Day 18

Again he prayed. (James 5:18)

There is a God in heaven who directs our steps, who prepares good works, who causes all things to work together for good, who fights our battles for us! These are all biblical truths. So even if it seems like God isn't answering your prayers, don't lose heart. Don't lose hope. Don't lose faith.

God rarely does things how or when we expect him to, and that leads us to question his strange and mysterious ways. I'm sure the Israelites questioned God's battle plan at Jericho. They would have preferred to storm the gates or scale the walls, but God told them to circle the city for seven days. It didn't make any sense. They must have felt foolish. It probably seemed like forever. But they kept circling!

Sometimes God will push us to our limits—the limits of our faith, of our patience, of our gifts. That is how God stretches our faith. We learn to listen closer to the Holy Spirit, to draw closer to our Savior, to lean harder on God.

If the Israelites had stopped circling Jericho, they would have lost what turned out to be their first victory in the promised land. But there was much more at stake than that: they would have lost the promised land altogether. However, the Israelites didn't stop. They listened to God, and they kept circling. And if you keep circling, the walls will come down. If you pray through, there will be a breakthrough.

I'm here, Lord. I'm listening. Lead me in the way I should go. Even when I'm tired or feeling impatient, I will keep praying.

Prayers I'm Circling

....

....

....

....

....

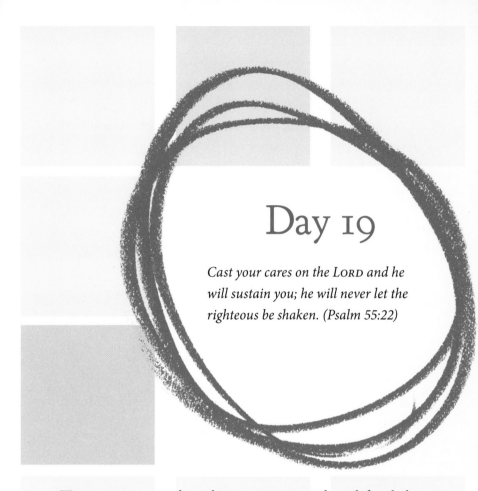

Day 19

Cast your cares on the LORD and he will sustain you; he will never let the righteous be shaken. (Psalm 55:22)

Jesus spent more than thirty years on earth and faced the same pressures and temptations that we do. He cried when his friend died (and then he brought that friend, Lazarus, back from the dead). He was angry at the dishonesty of the world (and turned tables of the money changers in the temple). He had anxiety about what was to come (and then he submitted to the cross).

He also had the perfect relationship with his heavenly Father. Jesus met God in prayer all the time. Because he prayed, Jesus was strong when he was tempted in the wilderness. Because he prayed, Jesus was tender and wise when he was with the hurting.

And because he prayed, Jesus taught others about thanking the Father, resisting the devil, and loving your neighbor.

Pray and rely on God like Jesus did when he was on earth. Worried about your math test? Let him know and ask him what you should do now. Not ready for your piano recital? Look for peace in him so you can be relaxed. Found out your friend cheated on a test, and you're not sure what to do? Cast your cares on God. He can't be rattled. He's not surprised. And he's completely by your side.

Lord, what would I do without you? Thank you for your example on earth, Jesus. I want to follow you.

Prayers I'm Circling

....

....

....

....

....

....

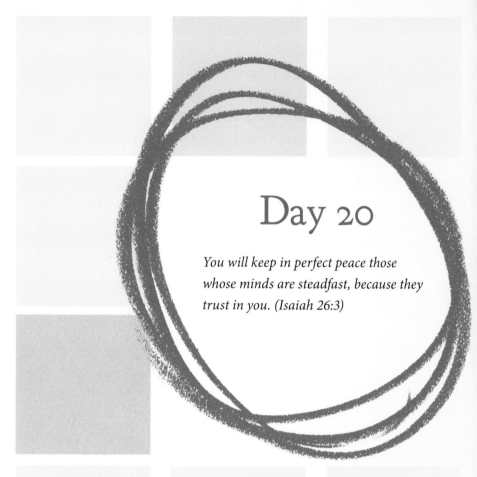

Day 20

You will keep in perfect peace those whose minds are steadfast, because they trust in you. (Isaiah 26:3)

S ometimes the purpose of prayer is to get us *out* of tough situations, but more often than not, the purpose of prayer is to help us *through* them. Should we pray for relief? Absolutely. But there are times we need to ask God to give us the willpower to keep on keeping on. For example, should you pray for Gramma and ask that she be cured from cancer? Yes! But you might also pray for God's grace to help her endure it. Should you ask to be rescued from the bully? Definitely! And you can pray for the strength to stand firm.

There is a big difference between praying *away* and praying *through*. We're often so anxious to get out of difficult, painful, or challenging situations that we fail to grow through them. We overlook the lessons God is trying to teach us. We fail to develop the character God is trying to grow in us. We're so focused on God changing our *circumstances* that we never allow God to change *us*!

There are situations when we need to pray through. Even when a prayer isn't answered the way we want, we have a peace that goes beyond our understanding because we know that God heard us. We praise God not just when his answer is yes but also when his answer is no. Can our prayers change our circumstances? Absolutely! But when our circumstances don't change, it's often an indication that God is trying to change us. Sometimes God delivers us from our problems; sometimes God delivers us through our problems.

Lord, you hear my prayers. You know my circumstances. You see me. No matter how you answer my prayer, may you be glorified, and may I see the ways you're helping me through.

Prayers I'm Circling

....

....

....

....

....

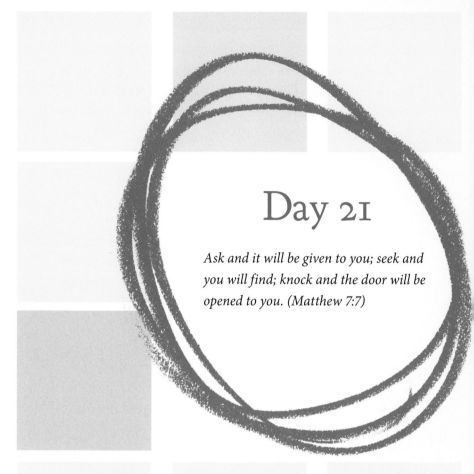

Day 21

Ask and it will be given to you; seek and you will find; knock and the door will be opened to you. (Matthew 7:7)

Ask. Seek. Knock. These aren't things we do once. They are actions that are repeated over and over again. Believers don't get discouraged if prayers seem to go unanswered. Jesus himself says to keep asking, keep seeking, keep knocking. It's an instruction every single child of God can obey.

The beauty of obedience is this: it relieves us of responsibility. It takes all the pressure off us and places it squarely on God's almighty shoulders. When we pray, we let go of control and worry and let God deal with our concerns in his all-knowing, all-loving wisdom. In prayer and obedience, we admit that he can handle everything we give to him.

Sometimes we're afraid of praying for miracles because we're afraid that God won't answer. But the answer isn't up to us. We never know if the answer will be yes, no, or not yet. It's not our job to answer; it's our job to ask.

That means you can take confidence in doing your "job" and presenting your requests to God. He is happy to receive all your worry, anxiety, hopes, dreams, and confessions over and over again.

I trust in you, Jesus, so I'm going to ask even if I've already asked for the same thing before. I'm going to confess the same sin for as long as it takes. I'm going to keep coming to you in faith that you hear all my requests.

Prayers I'm Circling

....

....

....

....

....

....

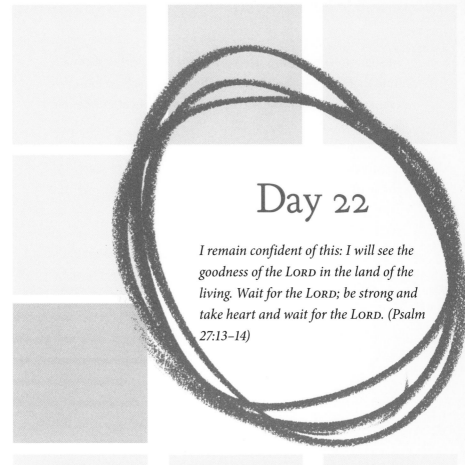

Day 22

I remain confident of this: I will see the goodness of the LORD in the land of the living. Wait for the LORD; be strong and take heart and wait for the LORD. (Psalm 27:13–14)

Think of all the waiting you do in a week: waiting for dinner, waiting for the bus, waiting in line at the store, waiting for your teacher or your mom or your little sister. It might feel some days like waiting is all you do!

Life is full of waiting, which is pretty boring and kind of hard. Waiting on the Lord can be especially hard, because it feels like time has slowed down and the Lord has moved on. Maybe there's something you've been asking him about for a long time. You might have prayed about a friend who's sick, or your grades that won't come up (no matter how hard you study), or your parents who just won't stop fighting. You've waited patiently, and you're still waiting!

In the Bible, God sometimes answers prayers by saying "wait." The Israelites waited to be rescued from Egypt, but they kept praying. Elijah waited in the cave for rain, but he kept praying. Paul waited in prison, but he kept praying.

In your prayer journal, list one thing you're waiting for God to do in your life. Next to that write, "God is with me." You might not have an answer just yet, but you never wait alone.

Thank you for taking care of me, Lord. Help me be patient while I wait for you.

Prayers I'm Circling

....

....

....

....

....

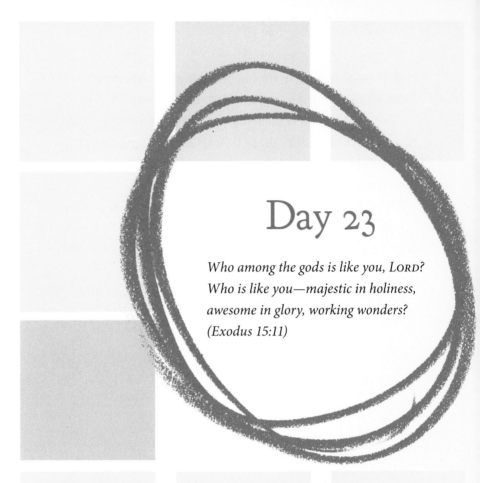

Day 23

Who among the gods is like you, LORD?
Who is like you—majestic in holiness,
awesome in glory, working wonders?
(Exodus 15:11)

Truth, love, and grace are revealed in the presence of God. Prayer takes you there. So get into God's presence. That is the solution to every problem. That is the answer to every question.

God wants to meet you at your best and at your weakest, at your saddest and at your happiest, at your most broken and at your most hopeful. That means you can get on your knees and trust him to do what only he can. If we get on our knees, the Holy Spirit will do the heavy lifting. If we get on our knees, the Holy Spirit will reveal things that can only be discovered in the presence of

God. If we get on our knees, the Holy Spirit will give us God-ideas for our lives.

Are your problems bigger than God, or is God bigger than your problems? Often, our real problem is our small view of God. Until we embrace the fact that God's grace and God's power know no limits, we will draw small prayer circles. But once we embrace the fact that God is powerful, we'll draw much wider circles around our God-given, God-sized dreams.

How big is your God? Is he big enough to heal your body, soothe your worries, and change your heart? Is he bigger than your worst sin, greatest fear, or biggest dream? If he is bigger than all those things, then pray like it.

Lord, I admit it's hard to imagine how great you are. My mind can't always picture the limitless power and love you have for me. I pray for some big, God-sized things and look for your answer.

Prayers I'm Circling

....

....

....

....

....

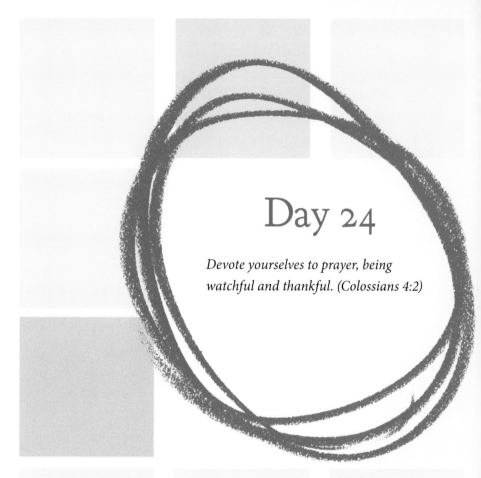

Day 24

Devote yourselves to prayer, being watchful and thankful. (Colossians 4:2)

The word *watchful* is a throwback to the practice of sitting on a city wall and keeping watch. Watchmen were the first ones to see attacking armies or traveling traders. They had the best view. They saw things no one else saw. They saw things before the rest of the city saw them.

This is precisely what happens when we pray. We see things no one else sees. We see things before others see them. We become God's watchmen. Prayer gives us a God's-eye view.

When you pray for someone or something, you start noticing anything related to those prayers. Have you ever noticed that when you pray, coincidences happen? It's more than chance; it's

God's hand at work. Prayer opens our eyes to see the ordinary miracles that surround us, the ordinary miracles that *are* us.

Like Jacob, we come to the ultimate realization: "Surely the LORD is in this place, and I was not aware of it" (Genesis 28:16). When we pray, we start seeing God everywhere we look. We see God in others. We see God's fingerprints on his creation. We see God-ordained opportunities all around us all the time. It's like what happens when we watch a film with 3-D glasses; when we pray, God comes toward us in surprising ways. Time to put on your spiritual 3-D glasses!

I want see the world through your eyes. Help me see the world the way it should be seen!

Prayers I'm Circling

....

....

....

....

....

....

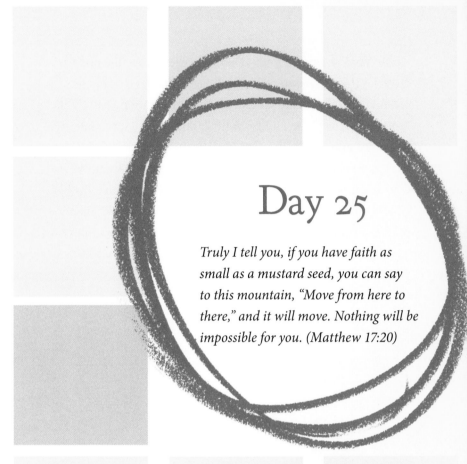

Day 25

Truly I tell you, if you have faith as small as a mustard seed, you can say to this mountain, "Move from here to there," and it will move. Nothing will be impossible for you. (Matthew 17:20)

If we are going to understand the potential of faith, we have to understand the power of a seed. Jesus spoke of our faith in relation to a mustard seed, the smallest seed in Israel's culture. Like every seed, it needs to take root and sprout. A mustard seed can take up to ten days to sprout, but some plants, like some dreams, take a lot longer. Faith is what keeps dreams alive, even when it seems as though they are dead and buried. But that is the very nature of seeds: They go underground. They disappear. And while it may seem like they are dead, they are not. They're just working beneath the surface!

If you saw a mustard seed but didn't know what it was, you would have a hard time imagining what it could become. The great potential is disguised in a tiny package. You would have no idea what the seed would grow to become or how big it could get. Faith is a lot like that. It doesn't look like much, but we never know what it can become.

A little faith goes a long way; in fact, a little faith will last an eternity.

Plant a seed of faith in my heart, Lord, so I can grow in you and bloom in front of others.

Prayers I'm Circling

....

....

....

....

....

....

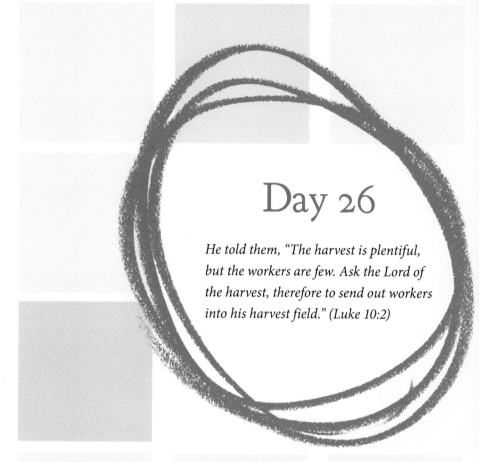

Day 26

He told them, "The harvest is plentiful, but the workers are few. Ask the Lord of the harvest, therefore to send out workers into his harvest field." (Luke 10:2)

Praying is planting. Each prayer is like a seed that gets planted in the ground. It disappears for a season, but it eventually bears fruit that blesses future generations. In fact, our prayers bear fruit even after we die. Each prayer takes on an eternal life of its own.

Isn't it true that we like things to happen at the speed of light instead of the speed of a seed planted in the ground? We want our dreams to become reality overnight. We want our prayers answered immediately. But that isn't the way it works.

We cannot make things grow. All we can do is plant and water. But if we pray as regularly as we would water a seed, God promises growth. If you sow kindness, you will reap kindness. If you sow generosity, you will reap generosity. If you sow love, you will reap love. After all, no farmer would plant beans and expect to harvest corn!

Sometimes it seems like the harvest will never come. And the temptation is to stop planting. Keep praying, keep obeying, keep giving, keep loving, keep serving. And if you keep sowing the right seeds, the harvest of blessing will come in God's time, in God's way! If we do the little things like they are big things, then God will do the big things like they are little things.

I will focus on daily prayer so that the harvest will be yours, Lord. Give me patience so I don't try to hurry the process.

Prayers I'm Circling

....

....

....

....

....

....

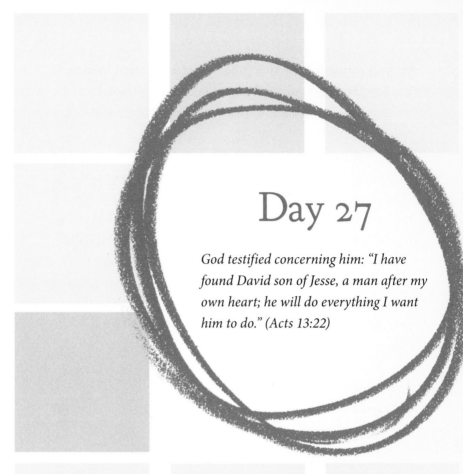

Day 27

God testified concerning him: "I have found David son of Jesse, a man after my own heart; he will do everything I want him to do." (Acts 13:22)

Have you ever read the King James Version of the Bible? Sometimes it's hard to understand because it uses words that people don't speak anymore. Words like *thee, thou,* and *thine* sprinkle the pages like glitter on a Christmas card. When you read God's Word in this version, thou soundeth like thou speaketh another language altogether! "How great Thou art?" Good question . . . if I could understand it!

God listens more to our hearts than to our words. Fine, fancy language is nothing compared to a heart that longs to be close to God. King David made plenty of mistakes, but he was a man after God's own heart. He loved God and praised him with worship and obedience.

At the same time, simple, sincere faith gets God's attention more than "thy" vocabulary. If you have a childlike faith, you take your heavenly Father at his word. You believe what he says. You trust that he is bigger than your problems, bigger than your mistakes, bigger than your dreams . . . because he says he is.

Don't be distracted by little things and outer appearances. God looks at the invisible—thy heart and thy faith.

I praise your holy name. Open my heart to you and grow my faith. I love you.

Prayers I'm Circling

....

....

....

....

....

....

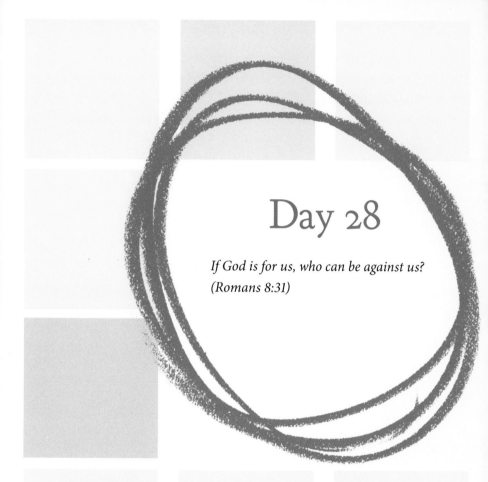

Day 28

If God is for us, who can be against us?
(Romans 8:31)

Instead of letting your circumstances come between you and God, let God come between you and your circumstances. Of course it's important to talk to God about your problems, but it's also important to talk to your problems about your God.

How do you start? You do the same thing that Jesus did when Satan tempted him in the wilderness. Jesus used the Word of God like a skilled swordsman. Satan had no chance. So as a prayer warrior yourself, start by writing down God's Word—verses like Philippians 4:13 ("I can do all this through him who gives me strength") and Romans 8:28 ("And we know that in all things God works for the good of those who love him, who have been called according to his purpose"). When you stand on God's Word, you can confidently proclaim God's truth.

Say someone bullies you at school. That's a serious problem that needs serious action, right? Take your problem to the Lord, who gives comfort and wisdom. He might remind you to tell grown-ups who have your back. And he might address the bully directly without you ever knowing. Don't forget that not even a stubborn bully can withstand the power of God!

Lord, you are my Savior. There is none like you. Thank you for your promises and faithfulness. I give my problems to you, and I give you to my problems.

Prayers I'm Circling

....

....

....

....

....

Day 29

Awake, and rise to my defense! Contend for me, my God and Lord. (Psalm 35:23)

In this Psalm, David is praying for God to take on his enemies. "Take up shield and armor," he writes. "Arise and come to my aid." David is looking for reassurance that God has his back. David knows that whether the battles are physical or verbal, God contends—or fights—for his children.

God is like the mama grizzly that protects her cubs. Since we are God's children, if anyone messes with us, they are messing with our heavenly Father. Long before we woke up this morning and long after we go to sleep tonight, the Holy Spirit was and is circling us in prayer. And if that doesn't give us holy confidence, I don't know what will.

You, too, can confidently call on God to come to your aid. If someone accuses or criticizes you, it's easy to get defensive or angry. Maybe someone spreads a rumor about you at school or your brother tells on you. The natural reaction might be to lash out and hit back with your own accusations. But remember God is contending for you. Pray to him. If you need forgiveness, ask God for it. If you need correction, be open to it. If your heart is in the right place, God will surely be more than happy to listen.

Lord, I know I'm not alone. Protect me when enemies come. Help me to answer criticism with wisdom. If words are meant to help me, let me be open to help. If words are meant to hurt me, protect me.

Prayers I'm Circling

....

....

....

....

....

....

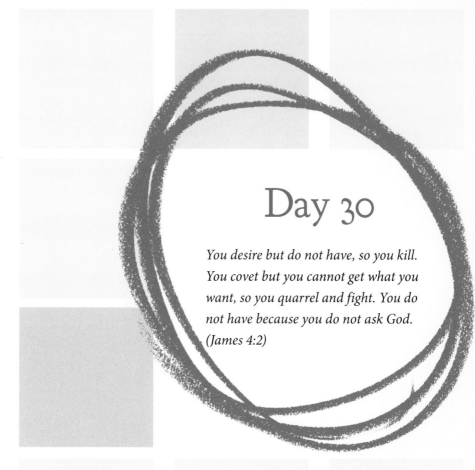

Day 30

You desire but do not have, so you kill. You covet but you cannot get what you want, so you quarrel and fight. You do not have because you do not ask God. (James 4:2)

What do you do every day? Roll out of bed. Eat breakfast. Brush your teeth. Talk to your family. Go outside. Do you pray as predictably as you get out of bed in the morning? Do you get your spiritual bread as daily as you get your toast at breakfast? Do you talk to God as much as you talk to your mom?

God delights in connecting with his children. Even in the beginning, he set it up so Adam and Eve had a relationship with him. But often we choose to ignore the invitation to get close to him. We insist on going it alone. But when we skip prayer, we set ourselves up for failure.

You don't have to worry if your prayers are long or short, elaborate or simple, public or private. *You* are enough. Maybe start with, "Lord, here I am!" and then listen. Move toward God and he will move toward you. Maybe pray, "What now?" and then wait for an answer. Maybe pray, "Lord, surprise me," and then watch for something extraordinary—something that you could not take credit for or control. No matter *how* you start, *start*. And know that God hears you and answers prayers a thousand times in a thousand ways!

Lord, here I am.

Prayers I'm Circling

....

....

....

....

....

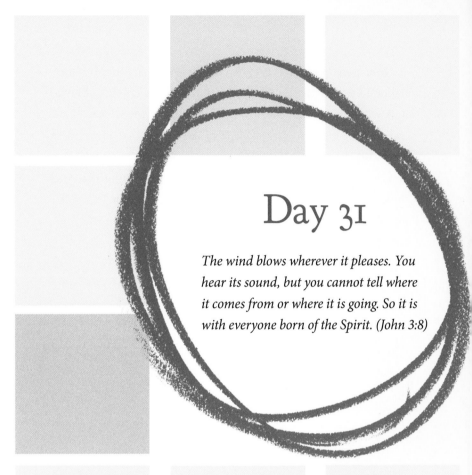

Day 31

The wind blows wherever it pleases. You hear its sound, but you cannot tell where it comes from or where it is going. So it is with everyone born of the Spirit. (John 3:8)

Here's a fun tongue twister: You can't never always sometimes tell. What does this mind-bender mean? Anything could happen!

When you circle a promise in prayer, you can't never always sometimes tell. Anything could happen. You never know when or how or where God will answer. Prayer adds an element of surprise to life that can knock your socks off.

Jesus refers to the Holy Spirit as wind. This is a great description of the way the Holy Spirit works. No one can see or control the wind, but it clearly moves with force and flexibility. It can be faint or strong, quiet or loud, soothing or unsettling. So it is with the Holy Spirit. One thing is certain: if we follow Jesus, our lives will be anything but boring.

God is trustworthy and unchanging. Even though God sometimes works in surprising ways, he will *always* be there for you. As a Christian, you can expect the unexpected because God is predictably unpredictable. You can't never always sometimes tell. Anything could happen!

Thank you, God, that I can count on you. Thank you for who you are—both dependable and exciting. I'm glad you work in amazing ways.

Prayers I'm Circling

....

....

....

....

....

....

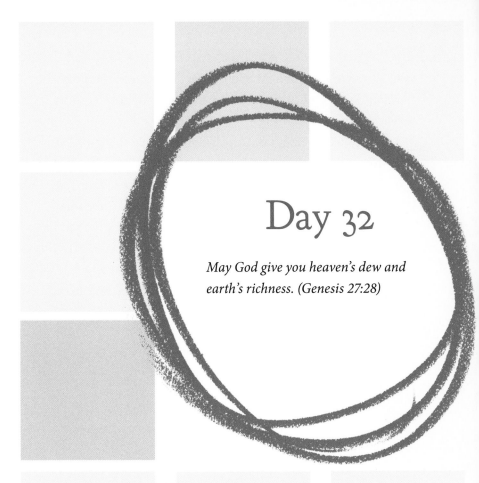

Day 32

May God give you heaven's dew and earth's richness. (Genesis 27:28)

God wants to bless you. That is, he wants to both lift you up and draw you closer to him. God is so creative and could bless you with anything—an answer to prayer, an idea or a dream you've had, an unexpected note from a friend, or a laughing fit with your sister. Maybe you don't *feel* blessed at the moment, because you're struggling with math or you lost your violin. But if you look around, you will find more blessings than you can count!

While sometimes God does bless us with things (earth's richness), other times he chooses to bless us with himself (heaven's dew). If you have accepted the gift of knowing Jesus, you've been blessed with the most important thing of all. In Philippians 4:12, Paul explains that he has learned to have peace in all things because he has Jesus. "I know what it is to be in need, and I know what it is to have plenty. I have learned the secret of being content in any and every situation, whether well fed or hungry, whether living in plenty or in want." Sometimes he had earth's richness and sometimes he didn't, but because he had Jesus, he had the greatest blessing of all.

I will write down my blessings in my journal every day. Then I can keep track of them, hunt for even more, and focus on your faithfulness. Blessing number one: The gift of Jesus, who is with me even now.

Prayers I'm Circling

....

....

....

....

....

....

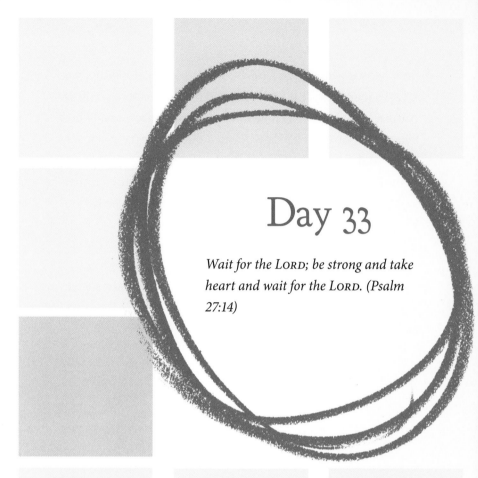

Day 33

Wait for the LORD; be strong and take heart and wait for the LORD. (Psalm 27:14)

Too often we pray ASAP prayers—as soon as possible. We need to start praying ALAT prayers—as long as it takes. Very rarely are our prayers answered as quickly or easily as we'd like. It's important to remember that God is never early. God is never late. God is always right on time.

It's tempting to attach an ASAP to every prayer, hoping that God will answer as soon as possible. But it's important to slow down and know God's timing is best for everybody. Rushing for an answer doesn't encourage patience or dependence on God. I don't want easy or quick answers because sometimes I take the credit for them, or I take them for granted. Don't look for the easiest path for you; look for the path that leads others to Jesus. It requires lots of circling. But the prayers you pray when you feel like you want to quit praying can bring the greatest breakthroughs.

What have you been circling in prayer? Maybe you've gotten a yes, a no, or a not yet. You've got to praise God if the answer is yes and trust him if the answer is no. If the answer is not yet, you've got to keep circling. It's always too soon to give up! What other option do you have? To pray or not to pray. Those are the only options.

Lord, I know you hear my prayers and know my heart. Help me be patient so I hear your voice and wait for your answers.

Prayers I'm Circling

....

....

....

....

....

....

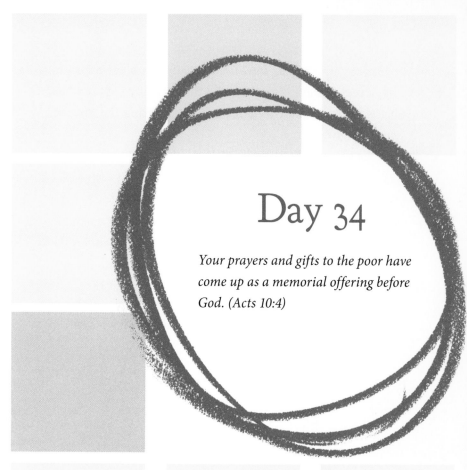

Day 34

Your prayers and gifts to the poor have come up as a memorial offering before God. (Acts 10:4)

Our nation's capital, Washington D.C., is filled with stone statues of former presidents, walls with names thoughtfully carved in them, and the gravestones of soldiers that mark their sacrifice for the country. Nearly six million people visit the Lincoln Memorial every year. They gaze at the face of his marble statue. They read his words etched in the walls. They cross over a memorial stepping stone where Martin Luther King Jr. stood to deliver his "I Have a Dream" speech. They look across the reflecting pool to the Washington Monument that stands like a rocket to heaven. Walk along these memorials, and it's impossible to forget our country's long history and the battles won along the way.

Every prayer we whisper is like the marble stones used to build the Lincoln Memorial. When we pray, we are building a tribute to God. Our prayers keep our focus and give him praise. They help us remember the moments we have spent together and the battles won. They are treated with respect and dignity, like the monuments that grace the United States capital.

Pray sincerely from the heart and God will take it in like tourists take in beautiful monuments. Your prayers will not be forgotten. They will not go unanswered.

In honor of who you are and what you've done, I offer my prayers to you, Lord. My "memorial offerings" are presented with faith, love, trust, and thanksgiving. Thank you for accepting them.

Prayers I'm Circling

....

....

....

....

....

....

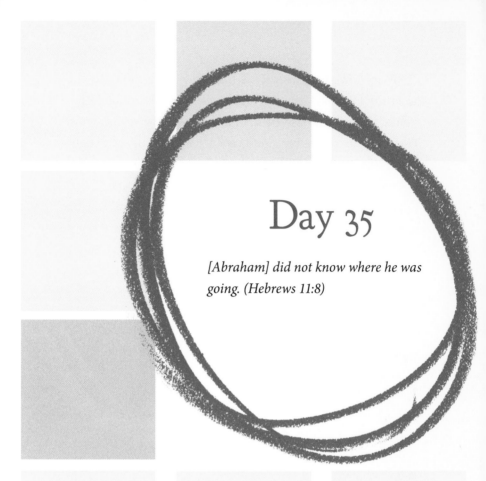

Day 35

[Abraham] did not know where he was going. (Hebrews 11:8)

It's hard to take a leap of faith. You'll never be completely ready. If you are looking for an excuse, you will always find one. If you feel like you never will be ready for anything God has called you to do, that's okay. God doesn't call the qualified; he qualifies the called. If you wait until you're ready, you'll be waiting for the rest of your life.

The author of Hebrews writes, "By faith Abraham, when called to go to a place he would later receive as his inheritance, obeyed and went, even though he did not know where he was going." Abraham didn't know the final destination, but it didn't keep him from taking the first step in the journey.

What's the next step you need to take in your journey? If you take the first step, God will reveal the second step. The problem is that most of us want to know the entire plan before we feel ready to step out in faith. We want to know exactly where we're going, but God doesn't operate that way. He gives us just enough direction, just enough grace, just enough strength to make a move. Why? So we will live in daily dependence on him. He doesn't want us to rely on ourselves; he wants us to rely on him.

Without knowing where he was going, Abraham took the first step, and God took care of the rest. God has a plan for you too. Don't wait until you feel old enough, wise enough, sure enough. You are exactly as ready as God wants you to be.

I depend on you, Lord, for direction and faith. I may not feel sure of my next step, but I feel sure of you. Thank you for leading me.

Prayers I'm Circling

....

....

....

....

....

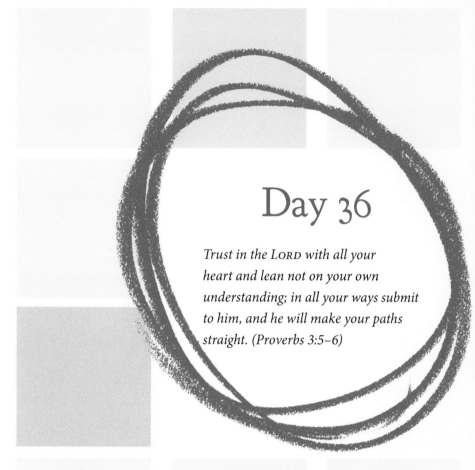

Day 36

Trust in the LORD with all your heart and lean not on your own understanding; in all your ways submit to him, and he will make your paths straight. (Proverbs 3:5–6)

Good things happen in the world all the time, but it's easy to be distracted by the bad things that happen too. On TV, in the news, and even in your own life, there seems to be bad news all around us.

When Adam and Eve disobeyed God in the garden of Eden, they introduced sin to God's perfect creation. Because of sin, there is brokenness in the world. But Jesus walks through the brokenness with us. You might wonder, *If he's so powerful, why doesn't he just fix it? Why did he allow it in the first place?* He's not offended by your tough questions. He's not upset with your pain and doubt. He's happy to give you comfort in prayer.

God is with you in bad news—whether it came on suddenly or slowly, whether you heard about it or caused it. Pray through your pain. He wants to help you carry it. Remember he is right with you. He has lived in this broken world too, and he knows how it goes. He is there to help you and keep you.

Lord, show me where to go and who to talk to when life gets painful. I'll start with you, because I know you are watching out for me.

Prayers I'm Circling

....

....

....

....

....

....

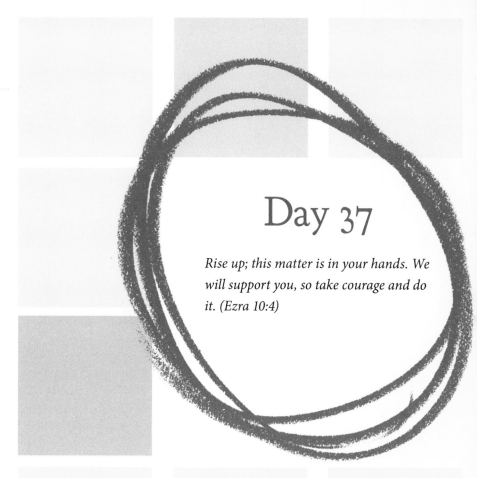

Day 37

Rise up; this matter is in your hands. We will support you, so take courage and do it. (Ezra 10:4)

Do you know the saying ready, set, go? It works great for races and games, but when it comes to faith, it's backward. The sequence of faith is this: go, set, ready. Some people spend their entire lives getting ready for what God wants them to do, but they never end up doing it because they never feel ready. This is where so many of us get stuck.

What if a new student came to your classroom? He looks different. His shoes are funny. His hair is messy. You know Jesus wants you to be a real friend to him, but you also know that others might look down on you the way they are looking down on him. It's going to take some courage to sit next to him at lunch. It's going to take grace to start a conversation and share a smile. Your actions may not work out the way you expect. You may get hassled, or he may change schools, or he may not be friendly. But you know Jesus, so you go be a friend. This is walking in faith.

If you are looking for excuses, you will always find one. Maybe you feel too young to make a difference. Maybe you feel too nervous to make a stand. Maybe you feel too shy to speak out. Faith is not faith until it is acted on. So go, set, ready!

Living in faith can be hard, especially when I am unsure. But I am sure of you, Lord. Be my courage, and lead me forward.

Prayers I'm Circling

....

....

....

....

....

....

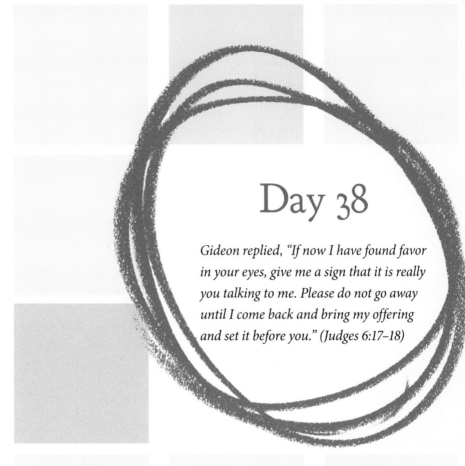

Day 38

Gideon replied, "If now I have found favor in your eyes, give me a sign that it is really you talking to me. Please do not go away until I come back and bring my offering and set it before you." (Judges 6:17–18)

When God called Gideon to become a judge in Israel, the young Israelite could hardly believe it. After all, the angel addressed him as "mighty warrior." I bet Gideon looked over his own shoulder to see who God was talking to, because there was no way it could be him! It sounded ridiculous. How could he, the least of his family, be a mighty warrior?

God answered, "I will be with you."

Gideon prayed and gave offerings. But still insecure, he needed more confirmation that he was correctly hearing from God himself. So he asked God if he could offer a test. Gideon put a wool fleece before the Lord and asked for a miracle—not once but twice!

Patiently, lovingly, God reassured Gideon.

To be clear, Gideon didn't ask God to *prove himself.* He wasn't being selfish or arrogant. He honored God with offerings first, and he followed God's directions. Then he asked for signs with genuine humility, an open heart, and a sincere faith.

And God reassured him, "I will be with you."

That's all we need to know, isn't it? God is with us, and God is for us. That is all you ever need to know. God is with *you*, and God is for *you*. Let that sink in!

Lord, who am I that you want to use me to accomplish your will? I feel small, but you are with me. Thank you, God, for your patience, reassurance, and comfort.

Prayers I'm Circling

....

....

....

....

....

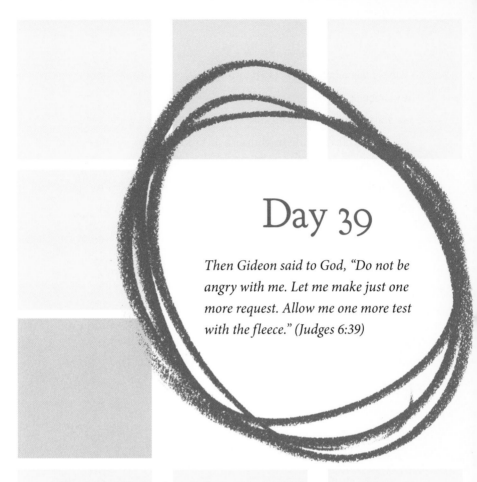

Day 39

Then Gideon said to God, "Do not be angry with me. Let me make just one more request. Allow me one more test with the fleece." (Judges 6:39)

In the book of Judges, Gideon asked God for a miraculous sign that involved a wool fleece. From this account, we get the term *prayer fleece,* which means asking God for a sign. Generally, signs don't go *before* our steps of faith; signs follow faith. But there are occasions when it's okay to ask God for confirmation if we aren't sure.

Here are a few cautions when it comes to "fleeces." First, if God has already answered your question in the Bible, then you don't need to even ask it. (For example, if you think God wants to treat you to a cookie on the down low from someone else's cookie jar, then look no further than the eighth commandment.) Second, check your motives to make sure they aren't selfish but are instead a genuine desire to honor God and do his will. (Again, sneaking a cookie in the name of God's will? . . . I don't think so.)

Here's a modern-day example. Anna was living her dream as a dancer when she got a clear impression she was supposed to use her gift for God. She wasn't sure what it meant, but she couldn't shake it. When she read about a ministry project in Serbia, something came alive in her spirit. That's when Anna put a "prayer fleece" before God: "Lord, if you want me to visit this ministry, then let me meet a Serbian this week." Anna shared her prayer fleece with her friends, and even though they thought it was a crazy prayer, they agreed to circle it with her. Two days later, a Serbian walked into her dance studio. She greeted him saying, "You're the one I've been waiting for!"

Lord, I have faith in you. I'm glad I can share my uncertainty with you, and you will communicate with me too.

Prayers I'm Circling

....

....

....

....

....

Day 40

You are my strength, I sing praise to you;
you, God, are my fortress, my God on
whom I can rely. (Psalm 59:17)

One of my prayer heroes is George Müller. Müller raised around 150 million dollars, but he didn't spend it on a mansion or a private jet or a three-level yacht. Instead he cared for 10,024 orphans while establishing 117 schools for their education throughout England.

Müller trusted God, so he turned every need into a prayer. When he needed a pipe fixed, he prayed for a plumber. When he needed food or money or books, he prayed that God would provide. It is estimated that more than thirty thousand specific prayers recorded in his journals were answered. (And just for the record, Müller read the Bible cover to cover more than two hundred times!) "I have known my Lord for fifty-seven years, and there is not one instance that I have failed to have an audience with the King," he once said matter-of-factly.

Müller wrote, "This is one of the great secrets in connection with successful service for the Lord; to work as if everything depended upon our diligence, and yet not to rest in the least upon our exertions, but upon the blessing of the Lord." The key to kingdom productivity is this: work really hard at what God has called you to do, but do not trust in your work; trust in God.

I want George Müller's confidence in prayer, and I want to do great things for you, Lord. I don't know what that looks like yet, but I'm glad that every time I pray, I know you are always listening.

Prayers I'm Circling

....

....

....

....

....

....

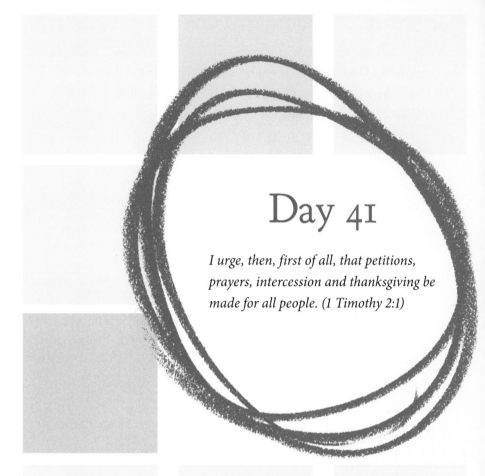

Day 41

I urge, then, first of all, that petitions, prayers, intercession and thanksgiving be made for all people. (1 Timothy 2:1)

Are you inspired to pray but don't know where to start? Try praying for the people God adores. That will give you plenty of inspiration. Pray for your family—the wisdom of your parents, the joy of your grandparents, the hearts of your brothers and sisters. Pray for those who are close to you—the relationships with your friends and jobs of your teachers. Pray for people even if you don't know their names—the waitress who serves your food, the janitor who cleans your school, the checker who bags your groceries.

And don't stop there.

Pray for the people who are hard to get along with. Get used to blessing their day with prayer. That means praying that they would know God's goodness that day. If your cousin teases you, bless his day with prayer. If your dad corrects you, bless his day with prayer. Even if someone rejects you, argues with you, or insults you, bless his day with prayer. If you pray this way, *you* will be the one blessed by prayer. Because it's impossible to spend that kind of time praying and not have your heart changed. You will become kinder, tougher, wiser, more patient, and more loving when you learn to see people from God's view.

Lord, I want to share your good news, so I will start with prayer.

Prayers I'm Circling

....

....

....

....

....

....

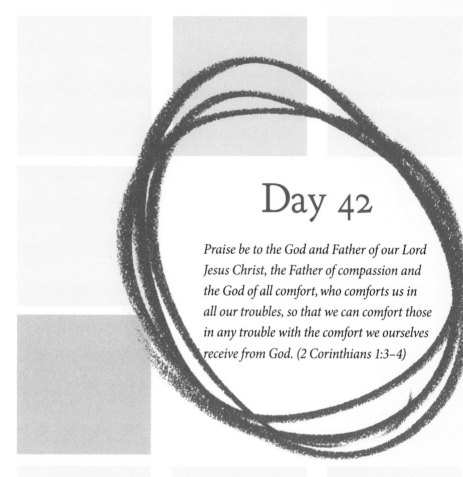

Day 42

*Praise be to the God and Father of our Lord
Jesus Christ, the Father of compassion and
the God of all comfort, who comforts us in
all our troubles, so that we can comfort those
in any trouble with the comfort we ourselves
receive from God. (2 Corinthians 1:3–4)*

God is Lord over each galaxy and every individual. He is
Lord above every country as well as every heart. He sees
the big picture and knows each personal story.

His "bigness" is matched only by his nearness. Because he
sees you, knows you, and loves you, he also knows your happi-
ness and your sadness. It's easy for us to be happy, but it isn't
always easy when we're sad, hurt, or lost. The great thing is, no
amount of pain is too much for the God of *all* comfort. So if your
best friend moves away or your dog passes away or your ankle
breaks, God can soothe your worry, calm your heart, and ease
your pain.

Draw circles around God's comfort by reading the Bible and then praying. Memorize verses like Isaiah 49:13: "Shout for joy, you heavens; rejoice, you earth; burst into song, you mountains! For the LORD comforts his people and will have compassion on his afflicted ones."

If you're sad, scared, or worried, you can bring it to your Savior in prayer. He knows how you feel. Start with a circle.

My heart is hurting, Lord. I need your love and comfort. Be close to me now.

Prayers I'm Circling

....

....

....

....

....

....

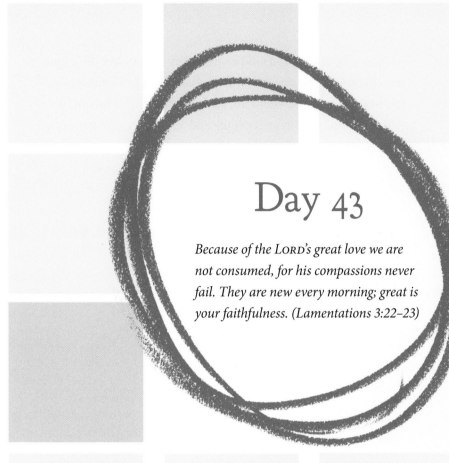

Day 43

Because of the LORD's great love we are not consumed, for his compassions never fail. They are new every morning; great is your faithfulness. (Lamentations 3:22–23)

A good place to start a meaningful prayer routine is by your bed. A good time to start is right away at the beginning of the day. Try this smooth move: Roll out of bed and onto your knees. Give God your first thoughts, your first words. It will set the tone for your entire day.

If you're a natural-born worrier, think of worry as a prayer alarm. Every time it goes off, pray. As you get in this habit, your worry will fade like steam from your cocoa. If you're a card-carrying doubter, take every hesitation as a cue to talk to God. He will crunch away your doubt like your morning cereal.

Remember this is the day that the Lord has made. As you

look out the window, thank him for each piece of creation you see. When you go school, tell him about all your cares. Before you start soccer or violin practice, lift up your skills and attitude to him. And as you crawl in bed at night, thank him for the grace he showed to you during the day. Then roll over and puff up your pillow with a thankful "Amen."

I want to have a strong, close relationship with you, Lord. And that starts with prayer. I want to give you the first moments of my day and grow from there.

Prayers I'm Circling

....

....

....

....

....

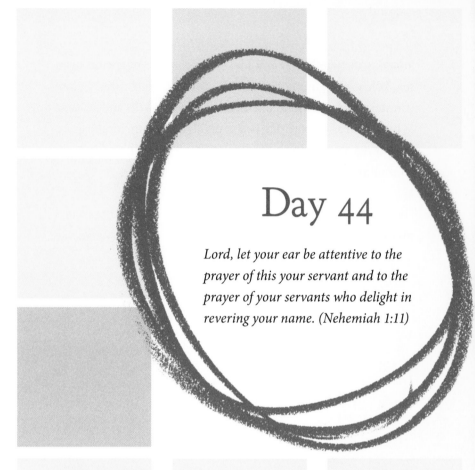

Day 44

Lord, let your ear be attentive to the prayer of this your servant and to the prayer of your servants who delight in revering your name. (Nehemiah 1:11)

No matter how far away you are from God, he is only one prayer away. You don't have to get on your knees or bow your head or fold your hands to be heard. Prayer isn't something you do with your eyes closed. Prayer is something you do with your heart open. It isn't a sentence that begins with "Dear Jesus" and ends with "Amen." In fact, some prayers don't involve words at all.

Your prayer might be a psalm from the Bible or a conversation as unique as the smile on your face. Your entire prayer might simply be, "Lord Jesus Christ, have mercy on me." Or it could last for hours. It could include requests *of* God or thank offerings *to* him. Your prayer might be anxious with worry or silent with reverence and respect.

Try experimenting with new prayer postures, like walking or kneeling. Try giving up your after-school TV on Mondays and replacing it with prayer. Try praying at different times, like when you shower or load the dishwasher. Create a gratitude list or a praise journal. If you want God to do something new in your life, don't do the same old thing. Do something different. Then see what a difference it makes!

I ask that my prayer life and relationship grow, like a garden of flowers. I will keep watering and tending to it, and you will help me bloom. Thank you, Lord.

Prayers I'm Circling

....

....

....

....

....

....

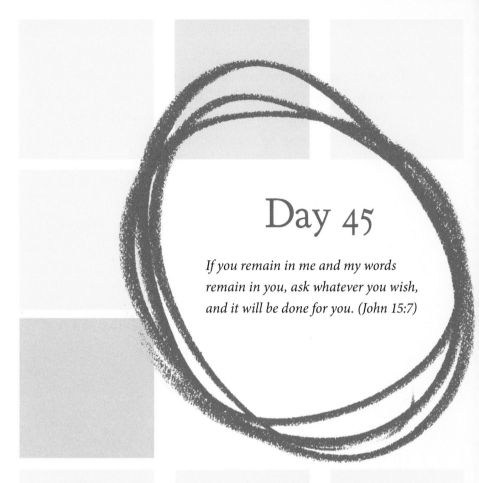

Day 45

If you remain in me and my words remain in you, ask whatever you wish, and it will be done for you. (John 15:7)

Try this: lie on your stomach on the floor. What do you notice? Maybe the soles of shoes. Maybe dust on the floor. Now stand on a chair and look around. From that height, you have a much wider view and can see a lot farther. Maybe you see the entire room. Maybe you spot a bird out a window. Just like when you stand on a chair, when you stand on the Word of God, you notice the world around you in a different light.

You're not going to read the Bible as fast as you would a comic book. In fact, the Bible wasn't meant to just be read. It was meant to be memorized and thought about. Words that are repeated throughout Scripture are God's way of saying, "Don't let this go in one ear and out the other." A story you learned in Sunday school at five years old becomes even more interesting at ten, at fifteen, at twenty-five!

Bible study is not something we start and stop like a vacation. It's something we do for the rest of our lives. It's like eating food that makes you feel good and strong. You wouldn't take just one bite and think, "I'm full! I'm done!" You'd finish the meal. You'd go back for seconds. You'd return the next day to get your fill and grow stronger.

I want to be close to you, Lord, so I will get close to your Word.

Prayers I'm Circling

....

....

....

....

....

....

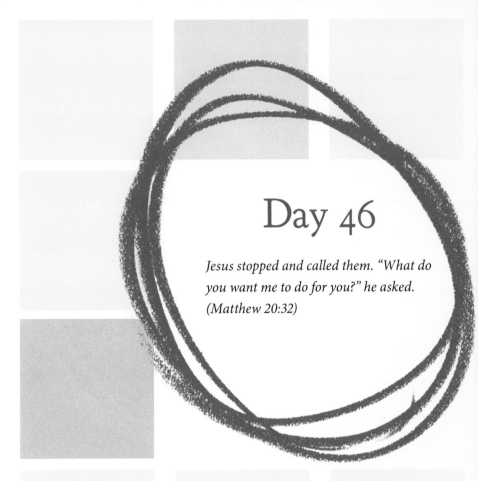

Day 46

Jesus stopped and called them. "What do you want me to do for you?" he asked. (Matthew 20:32)

More than a thousand years after Joshua won the battle at Jericho, another miracle happened in the same place. Jesus was on his way out of the city when two blind men shouted, "Lord, Son of David, have mercy on us!" (Matthew 20:30). The disciples saw it as a bother, but Jesus stopped and asked the two men a question: "What do you want me to do for you?"

Wasn't it obvious what they wanted? And didn't Jesus know everything anyway? Yet Jesus connected with them. He didn't heal them from a distance. He wanted to touch them personally. He wanted to make sure that *they* knew what they wanted from God. Did they want to be saved? They did. The Bible says, "Jesus had compassion on them and touched their eyes. Immediately they received their sight and followed him" (Matthew 20:34).

What if Jesus asked you the same question: *What do you want me to do for you?* Do you want to be saved so you can follow him? Are you at a loss for words? Most of us don't get what we want simply because we don't know what we want! We've never circled any of God's promises. And we've forgotten most of the prayers we've prayed before they are even answered. Pull out your journal and write down what's on your heart. If it's a prayer request, write down the date, so you can revisit it later and see where God has taken you.

Lord, I want to circle my prayers and see the things you've done for me. I can't wait to hear from you.

Prayers I'm Circling

....

....

....

....

....

....

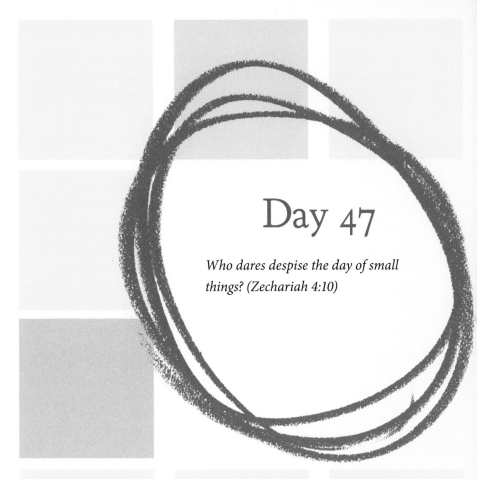

Day 47

Who dares despise the day of small things? (Zechariah 4:10)

On July 1, 1857, Jeremiah Lanphier became a city missionary in New York City. He began a daily meeting where business people could gather for midday prayer. Only six people showed up to the first meeting. The following week, there were fourteen. The week after that, there were twenty-three. The prayer meeting eventually outgrew the church itself. After that, the daily gatherings for prayer took place all over the city. One reporter visited twelve prayer meetings on one day and counted 6,100 men seeking God in prayer!

Who were those people at the first prayer meeting? Were they discouraged there were only six of them? Or did they see that God can make extraordinary things happen from the smallest steps of faith?

Don't judge your prayers by counting the number of people who agree with you, support you, stand with you, or cheer you on. You can't predict how God is going to grow your prayers and use your devotion. Your only concern is to be faithful. So relax and pray on. You've got to start somewhere, and God is in charge of the results. If you do little things, God will do the big things. Do your part, and be on the lookout for God to do his part.

Give me faith to follow you, Lord. I'll start with prayer and trust you for the results.

Prayers I'm Circling

....

....

....

....

....

....

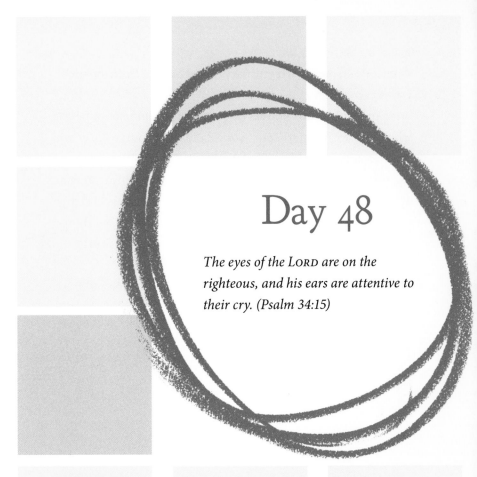

Day 48

The eyes of the LORD are on the righteous, and his ears are attentive to their cry. (Psalm 34:15)

The Bible says that God listens when his children pray. Sometimes, it's hard to believe. After all, we can't see him with our eyes or hear him with our ears. We have to take it on faith. That is, we believe that God listens even if it seems like he's on the other side of the galaxy.

If you've ever had trouble believing God hears you, you're not alone. There was a man in the Bible who told Jesus, "I do believe; help me overcome my unbelief!" (Mark 9:24). Jesus answered the man's spoken prayer with a miracle.

If you could see Jesus with your own eyes, you would know that he is with you right now. In fact, he's an expert on you. He knows your insides—your thoughts and secrets. And he knows your outsides—the stress at home, the pressure at school. And he loves you with a faithfulness you can count on. Since you can't see him, you'll need faith to believe it. If that's hard, tell him, "I believe. Help me overcome my unbelief." And he will.

Next time you're wondering if God is on another planet, forget about it. He will never abandon you. He sees, he hears, he listens. Believe it.

Lord, I circle your promise that you see me and listen to me. Help me to know I'm never alone. Help me with my faith and to know that you are here.

Prayers I'm Circling

....

....

....

....

....

....

Day 49

Be joyful in hope, patient in affliction, faithful in prayer. (Romans 12:12)

God sees our hope and our hurts, and he hears our prayers for both. He loves to work alongside his children to make dreams come true and make sadness fade away. Prayer is the key to it all.

Join with the Lord by getting on your knees as his humble servant. Ask for his involvement, his wisdom, his direction: Where does *he* want to work? What is *your* role to play? Maybe God will use you to share the good news with a friend. Maybe he wants you to be a leader in the classroom. Maybe he wants you to serve at home. Your heavenly Father cheers when you take even the smallest of steps in the right direction. Small steps—like being joyful in hope, patient in trouble, faithful in prayer—become long jumps in God's kingdom.

In this world, it's easy to get distracted from our holy purpose. Sometimes we get sidetracked from prayer. Maybe serving others starts to feel like a chore. Or maybe it feels like we're not doing *enough*. But doing ordinary things means cooperating with God, who does extraordinary things. So open your Bible. Bow your head. Listen for God's guidance. Remember: joyful, patient, faithful. Start with prayer and expect the ordinary to become extraordinary.

Lord, work in me so that I can work in the world.

Prayers I'm Circling

....

....

....

....

....

....

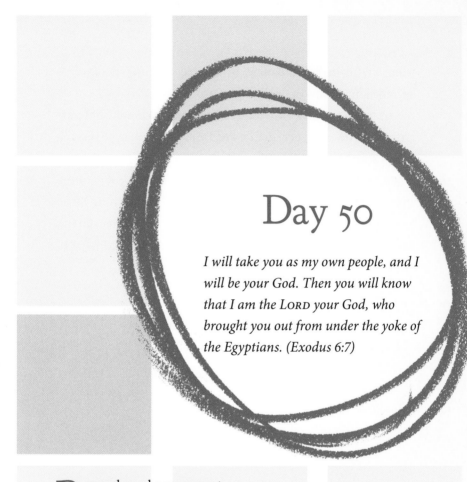

Day 50

I will take you as my own people, and I will be your God. Then you will know that I am the LORD your God, who brought you out from under the yoke of the Egyptians. (Exodus 6:7)

Remember who you pray to.

The Bible offers a lot of names for God, names that reveal who he is and what he does—the Lord Is Peace, the Most High God, the God Who Heals. He is Daddy. He is King. He is God With Us.

You have a standing invitation with this God of the Bible. You are welcome to talk to him directly, all the time. He isn't distant. He always has time for his special child—you.

The same God who created Adam, who rescued Joseph, who saved the Israelites, who led King David, who sent his only son . . . this is the same God you find in prayer. Prayer isn't just for people in the Bible, or missionaries in faraway places, or pastors on a stage. He is the God who sees children and grown-ups, new followers and old believers, the joyful and the broken-hearted. Have you answered his invitation to follow him?

Open the Bible and take God at his word. That means, read the words, believe what God says, obey, and pray.

My Father, thank you that I am as precious to you as King David was. It is wonderful that I can talk to you about my failures and my fears, my dilemmas and my dreams, and you always listen and answer.

Prayers I'm Circling

....

....

....

....

....

....

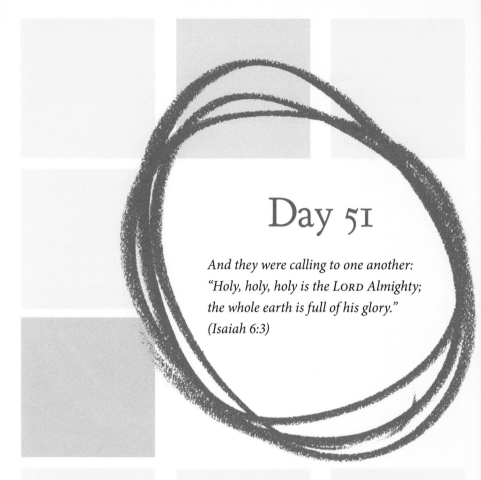

Day 51

And they were calling to one another:
"Holy, holy, holy is the LORD Almighty;
the whole earth is full of his glory."
(Isaiah 6:3)

When you think about God, what images come to mind? I picture Jesus with a lamb draped around his shoulders, because that is the painting that hung in my grandparents' house. For some people, the image might be Jesus hanging on a cross, especially like it's shown in a lot of churches. The perfect Son of God on the cross for our sins is a tragic and beautiful image of what true love looks like.

There is another way to picture Jesus: as he is now, no longer hurt and hanging on a cross but healed, whole, and sitting on a throne. In chapter 6 of Isaiah, the prophet reveals his vision of the Lord being praised. The train of Jesus' robe fills the temple, and angels fly above him proclaiming, "Holy, holy, holy is the LORD Almighty; the whole earth is full of his glory."

Don't accept a low, small view of God. He is so much better than our best thoughts. He is a shepherd tending to his sheep, a King over all the earth, a close daddy, a Savior for the entire world. He knows praise and sacrifice, joy and sorrow, temptation and victory. He is higher, closer, and more than we could ever dream.

That means you can take heart, have joy, and be confident, because your Father is wiser, more gracious, and more powerful than anything you can imagine.

I praise you, Lord. I know you are greater than a pillar of fire and closer than a father. I want to know you even more.

Prayers I'm Circling

....

....

....

....

....

....

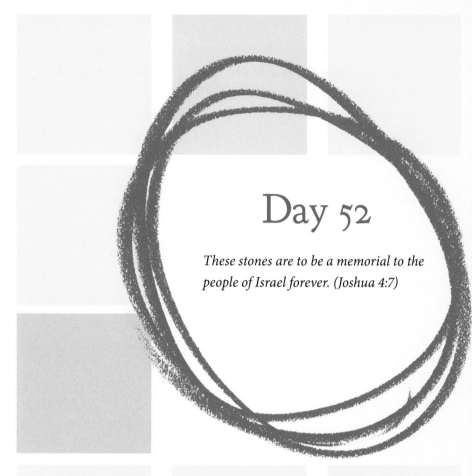

Day 52

These stones are to be a memorial to the people of Israel forever. (Joshua 4:7)

The Israelites built memorials where God showed his faithfulness to them. They would often return to those ancient altars to renew their relationship with God. Throughout history, and even today, people make pilgrimages—long trips—to visit amazing places in countries like Israel. Returning to places of spiritual meaning honors God for what he has done and reminds his children of his faithfulness.

Elijah couldn't return to Mount Carmel without remembering what God had done there. In a sudden-death showdown on the mountain, Elijah went head to head with 450 prophets of Baal. Elijah prayed for a miracle and God answered with fire.

Elijah went back to the mountain to pray for rain on a country that was in its fourth year of drought. No doubt Elijah prayed with confidence in the God he served. It's hard not to pray with faith when we pray in a place where God has already done a miracle.

When God answers your prayer, remember it: write about it in your prayer journal, paint a picture, find a special stone as a memorial. Do something special to mark the special something that God did with you.

Lord, you are faithful. I remember specific ways you have blessed me and answered my prayer. I want to be faithful to you.

Prayers I'm Circling

....

....

....

....

....

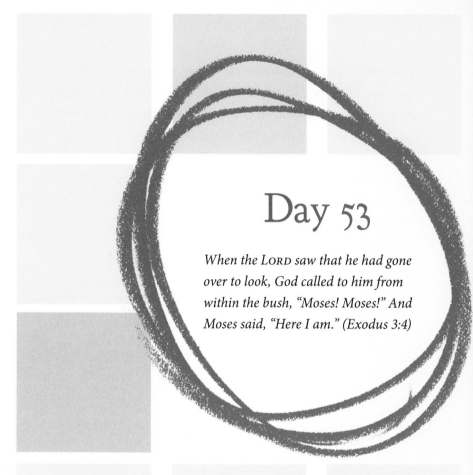

Day 53

When the LORD saw that he had gone over to look, God called to him from within the bush, "Moses! Moses!" And Moses said, "Here I am." (Exodus 3:4)

People like to finish—finish first, finish fast, finish well. We can't wait to finish our homework, finish the project, finish middle school. But the finish is only one small slice of the entire process. Slow, ordinary, daily practice is what makes a job well done.

Being faithful in the process is as important as what happens at the end. God uses everyday work and ordinary practice to shape us. Praying daily, getting along with others, being honest, working hard—all of these things are part of a godly life. It's not just about doing great things *for God*. It's also about God doing great things *in us*. And we shouldn't be in any rush to finish that!

Before leading the Israelites out of Egypt, Moses spent forty years as a shepherd in the desert. One day Moses got up, put on his sandals, picked up his staff, and started an ordinary day in an ordinary way. Then God appeared. The burning bush changed the course of his life (and the lives of every Israelite slave in Egypt). This was only the beginning of Moses' journey—there would be a long, hard road for him to take before his work was done!

No place is too distant, too out of the way, too unlikely for God. It doesn't matter where you are—God can meet you anywhere. But if you are rushing to finish something, you may miss God along the way. Practice making time every day to look for God with patience.

Lord, I want to pray daily. I want to say to you every day, "Here I am."

Prayers I'm Circling

....

....

....

....

....

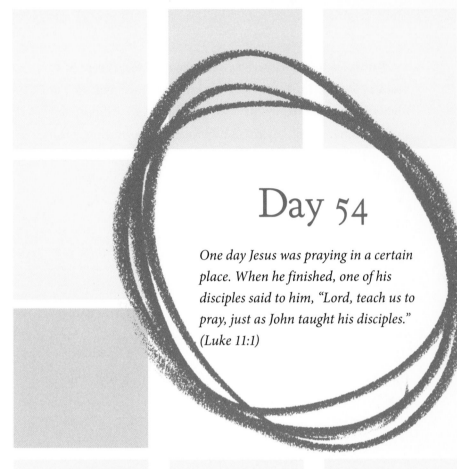

Day 54

One day Jesus was praying in a certain place. When he finished, one of his disciples said to him, "Lord, teach us to pray, just as John taught his disciples." (Luke 11:1)

A father walked by his daughter's bedroom one night and overheard her praying the alphabet. "Dear God, a, b, c, d, e, f, g . . ." She prayed all the way to z and said, "Amen."

"Sweetie," the dad said, "why were you praying that way?"

His daughter replied, "I didn't know what to say, so I let God put the letters together however he wants."

We all feel that way sometimes. We might feel like we don't have the exact right words. We might feel like hiding our troubles from God. Or we might feel too young to know what to say. We may simply just not know where to start.

Try praying about what to pray about. If you get stuck, go

back to the Bible. Start reading, and God will start speaking. Words, phrases, or verses will stand out to your spirit. That's when you stop reading and start praying.

Use your prayer journal to write out a verse. Then take a second to think about it. Did someone come to mind? Did you feel hopeful, encouraged, or challenged when you read it? Can you see how a truth in the Word might apply to your life at home? For example, "Love your neighbor" (Matthew 22:39) might remind you of your friend across the street who hurt your feelings. Pray about that problem and how you might forgive him. Pray for him. Pray that he would notice God's grace that day.

Get a pen, grab your prayer journal, open God's Word, and never have to pray the ABCs again.

Lord, thank you for your Word that shows me who you are and how to pray.

Prayers I'm Circling

....

....

....

....

....

Day 55

*All this is for your benefit, so that
the grace that is reaching more and
more people may cause thanksgiving
to overflow to the glory of God.
(2 Corinthians 4:15)*

God knows his children backward and forward. He knows all about your heart, habits, headspace, even your hair. ("And even the very hairs of your head are all numbered," Matthew 10:30). It's with delight in his children (in you!) that God keeps his promises, answers prayers, performs miracles. That is who he is. That is what he does.

When we draw a circle around the tough situations in our lives, we invite God to get involved. The impossible to us is possible to God. When God takes over and we know there is nothing we can do, we are reminded of his care and his control.

So if your mom needs treatment, or your grandma is sick,

or your dad is worried with work, or your teacher blames you, or your coach yells at you, or your dog bites you, or Bubba down the street steals your lunch money, you are only one prayer away from God's care and control. The bigger the problem, the bigger the circle we draw.

When was the last time you asked God for something and saw it answered? Every answered prayer is evidence of God's faithfulness. When the answers come, don't forget to write them down in your journal. The notes will boost your faith, set off praise, and encourage you to circle even more in prayer.

Thank you, Lord, for your promises. I'm relieved that I can always count on you.

Prayers I'm Circling

....

....

....

....

....

....

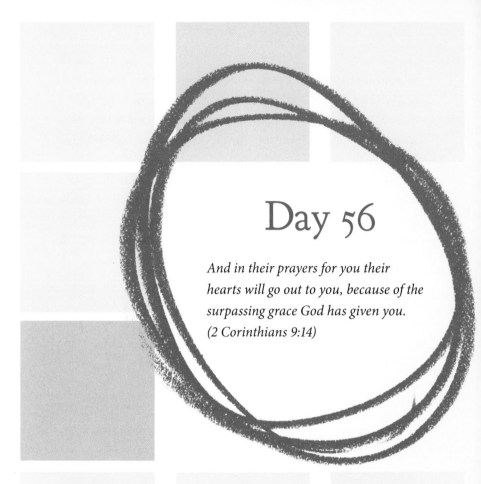

Day 56

And in their prayers for you their hearts will go out to you, because of the surpassing grace God has given you.
(2 Corinthians 9:14)

When you pray, do you think about God's goodness? You are getting stronger in hope. Do you thank him? You are developing a grateful spirit. Do you listen as much as you share? You are nurturing a strong relationship. Do you rely on him? You are gaining godly confidence.

The things you do and say are influenced by how you pray. The more you pray, the more your eyes are open to the work God's doing in you and around you. The more you confess your sins, the more you trust in God's good heart and forgiveness. The more you are forgiven, the more you forgive others. The more you talk to God, the more you think about him even when you're not praying.

Prayer changes you and how you look at the world. Tend to your heart by spending time with your God. How will you pray today?

Lord, help me make prayer into a habit so my hope, gratitude, and relationship with you will grow stronger.

Prayers I'm Circling

....

....

....

....

....

....

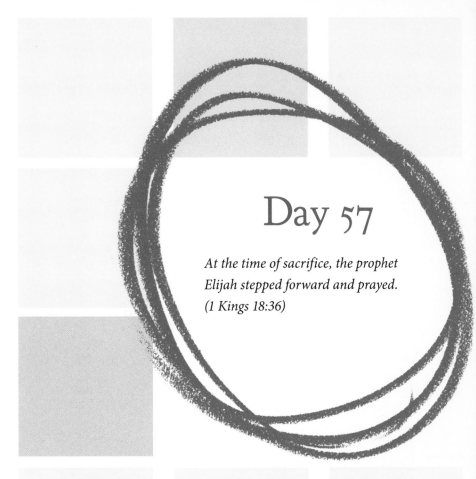

Day 57

At the time of sacrifice, the prophet Elijah stepped forward and prayed.
(1 Kings 18:36)

The Bible is filled with exciting stories. If it was a newspaper, you'd read sensational headlines like this:

Rain in Forecast: Local resident builds boat in desert (Genesis 6)

Giant Killed in Battle: Shepherd refuses armor before killing Philistine (1 Samuel 17)

Shipwreck!: Paul reports all 276 passengers survive (Acts 27:27–44)

Earthquake Rocks Prison: Apostles Paul and Silas remain uninjured (Acts 16:16–40)

There is a backstory behind every headline. The backstory is prayer.

Consider 1 Kings 18, when Elijah took on the prophets of Baal on Mount Carmel. The headline would mention the miracle: "Waterlogged Altar Goes Up in Flames!" The backstory is Elijah's prayer in verses 36 and 37: *"Lord, the God of Abraham, Isaac and Israel, let it be known today that you are God in Israel and that I am your servant and have done all these things at your command. Answer me, Lord, answer me, so these people will know that you, Lord, are God, and that you are turning their hearts back again."*

Elijah's prayer demonstrated his close relationship with the living God. And God answered with a miracle that is still spoken about today. We all have been invited to have a close relationship with the Lord. It starts with a simple prayer and grows from there.

There are a lot of big headlines in the Bible: pillars of fire, epic battles, evil kings, brave prophets, spies, secrets, betrayal . . . But don't overlook the quieter, powerful practice of prayer. It is the groundwork for the miracles.

Focus on the backstory of prayer, and God will write the headlines.

Lord, I want to know you well. I want to pray with confidence. I want to call on you in faith.

Prayers I'm Circling

....

....

Day 58

Give us each day our daily bread.
(Luke 11:3)

Manna was a mystery, a total unknown. Even its name, meaning "What is it?", showed that no one could figure it out. So God gave the Israelites some instruction . . . The "bread" from heaven will appear every morning and disappear by the afternoon, like dew. So get up and gather *just enough* for one day. Gather more and you'll have maggots in your manna the next morning. On the sixth day, though, gather just enough for two days, because there will not be any manna sent on the Sabbath.

Serious miracle, right? Every single day for forty years in the desert, God provided *just enough*. Why did he forbid leftovers?

What's wrong with planning ahead and gathering enough manna for a few days or a few weeks?

Manna was a daily reminder to the Israelites of their dependence on God. Remember, God wants a relationship with his children, and that means connecting every day—and not just for food. If the Israelites knew they could rely on him every day for their basic needs, God's hope was they might learn they could rely on him for their health, their courage, their dreams, their everything. Isn't that the point of the Lord's Prayer? "Give us each day our daily bread." We want a one-week or one-month or one-year supply of God's provision, but God wants us to drop to our knees every day in complete dependence on him.

Nothing has changed since the Israelites were rescued from slavery. God wants a relationship with *you*. He doesn't want you to go it alone and fend for yourself. He wants you to depend on him. And this starts with prayer.

Lord, thank you for providing for me. Please give me what I need today.

Prayers I'm Circling

....

....

....

....

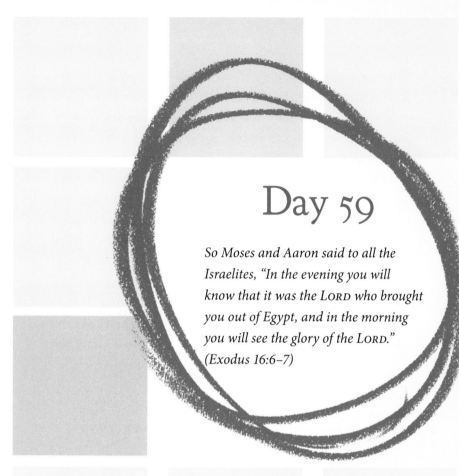

Day 59

So Moses and Aaron said to all the Israelites, "In the evening you will know that it was the LORD who brought you out of Egypt, and in the morning you will see the glory of the LORD." (Exodus 16:6–7)

From the moment he floated in a basket down the river to safety, Moses was set apart for divine plans. He marveled at a burning bush that didn't burn up (Exodus 3:2). He was on the front lines when God parted the Red Sea (Exodus 14:21). He ate miracle manna every day (Exodus 16:4).

As Moses witnessed God's miracles, he also heard the complaints of his people. As they followed God through the desert, the Israelites moaned, "I wish we had fish and vegetables like we used to eat in Egypt. Now all we ever see is this manna!" Even today God does wonders all the time, yet we still find something to complain about. Maybe God gave you a big brain, but you grumble about not running as fast as Billy Bobby Joe. It's sadly common to complain even as we receive gifts from God.

Despite the Israelites' complaints, God met their needs. He sent them quail to eat. He didn't promise a one-course meal of meat; he promised meat for a month. Even Moses could hardly believe it. He couldn't imagine how God could fulfill the impossible promise for a day, let alone a month. "Is the LORD's arm too short?" God responds. "Now you will see whether or not what I say will come true for you" (Numbers 11:23).

Remember the God who took care of the Israelites takes care of you. Don't forget how he provides.

Lord, I will draw a prayer circle around your blessings to me. That is, I will think on them over and over so I will never forget them. Then my faith will be strengthened and our relationship will grow.

Prayers I'm Circling

....

....

....

....

....

Day 60

Now a wind went out from the LORD and drove quail in from the sea. It scattered them up to two cubits deep all around the camp, as far as a day's walk in any direction. All that day and night and all the next day the people went out and gathered quail. (Numbers 11:31–32)

The Israelites had been witnessing God's miracles even before they entered the desert. They had short memories, though. Not long after God provided something, they complained about their lack of something else. When they moaned because they had no meat, God promised to answer by providing protein . . . for a whole month! Moses did the math. Had he heard God correctly? He couldn't even picture that much food.

The Israelites were parked in the Desert of Paran, fifty miles from the closest sea. Quail live by the water, and they don't fly long distances. But God sent a supernatural wind that blew the birds inland. The quail literally arrived at the feet of God's people. Quail fell from the sky like hail on an area that was ten times larger than our nation's capital. The quail were piled three feet deep as well. It was like a bird blizzard!

The quail are signs of God's generosity, patience, faithfulness, and care. Moses never could have anticipated this answer to prayer. Yet again, God responded with unexpected abundance.

Dear Lord, I know my job isn't to make sure your plans add up. Because I trust in you, I will pray faithfully. Maybe you will multiply the miracles in my own life.

Prayers I'm Circling

....

....

....

....

....

....

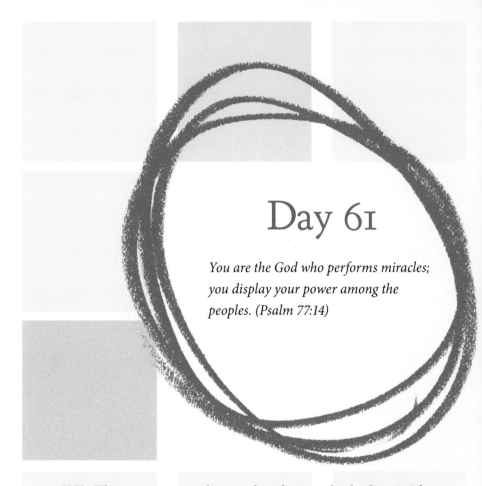

Day 61

You are the God who performs miracles; you display your power among the peoples. (Psalm 77:14)

When you write a letter, what do you think about? Of course you think through *what* you're going to write, but don't you also think about *who* you're writing to? A note to your great aunt is different than one to your best bud, which is different than one to your two-and-a-half-year-old cousin. Maybe everybody wants to hear about your trip to the amusement park, but who are you going to congratulate for using the potty like a big boy? Not your great aunt Sally! In all communication, *who* you're talking to matters!

When you're talking to God, it's important to know about him. His wisdom, power, and love is perfect. He sees everything, knows everything, rules over everything. He cares about all his creation, but he's especially fond of his children. He's especially fond of you. Who wouldn't want to talk to and rely on God in prayer?

Remember, the size of your prayers is nothing compared to the size of your God. If your god is small, you'll pray small prayers. But if your God knows no limits, then neither should your prayers. To God, everything is simple. When Jesus rose from the dead and walked out of the tomb, the word *impossible* was removed from the vocabulary of believers. God's not bound by anything, so maybe we should pray that way!

Don't forget this: an "impossible" prayer request keeps us on our knees in dependence on God. Drawing prayer circles around our dreams isn't just to accomplish great things for God; it also means God accomplishes great things in us.

I come to you in prayer, because of who you are—faithful and kind, powerful and tender. I'm so glad I can trust you.

Prayers I'm Circling

....

....

....

....

....

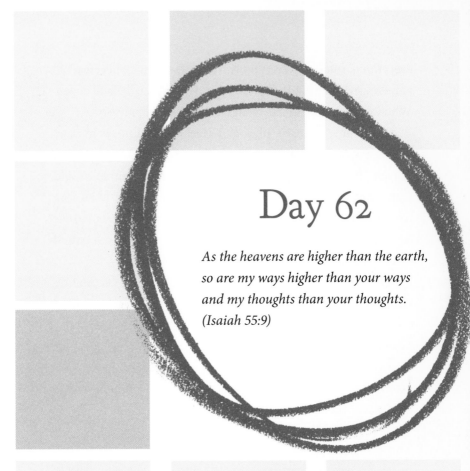

Day 62

*As the heavens are higher than the earth,
so are my ways higher than your ways
and my thoughts than your thoughts.
(Isaiah 55:9)*

Has your mom ever told you that she loved you "to the moon and back"? What does that mean? Earth is simply too small to contain her love, so she had to exit the atmosphere! She had to get spacy.

Isaiah gets spacy too. Earth is simply too small to contain God's love or his power or his presence. So Isaiah exits the atmosphere to give a glimpse of how big God is.

Check out this math: The sun is more than 94 million miles away from the earth. If you could drive to the sun traveling 65 miles per hour, 24 hours a day, 365 days a year, it would take you more than 163 years to get there. While 94 million miles may seem like a long distance by earthly standards, the sun is our next-door neighbor in space. The sun is the nearest star in our tiny little galaxy known as the Milky Way. There are more than 80 billion galaxies in the universe! Yet God says that this is the distance between his thoughts and our thoughts.

Forget the numbers. They are too big to really understand. And that's the point. We may not be able to picture him, but God has no limits. Numbers can't describe him. Time can't stop him. Space can't contain him. Remember this every time you feel overwhelmed by your problems or your sin or your future. Your God is bigger than them all.

Lord, I love you to the moon and back.

Prayers I'm Circling

....

....

....

....

....

....

Day 63

The LORD said to him, "Who gave human beings their mouths? Who makes them deaf or mute? Who gives them sight or makes them blind? Is it not I, the LORD? Now go; I will help you speak and will teach you what to say."
(Exodus 4:11–12)

When God appeared to Moses through the non-burning burning bush, Moses was stunned by the miracle. He was stunned by God's holy presence. And he was stunned by the call. "So now, go," God said. "I am sending you to Pharaoh to bring my people the Israelites out of Egypt" (Exodus 3:10).

This is how Moses basically responded: "Uhhh, excuse me?"

"I will be with you," God reassured him.

"But what if they wonder who sent me? . . . What if they don't believe me? . . . But I can't speak well . . . Maybe you could send someone else . . ."

Every single time Moses said, "Uhhh, who am I? I'm unqual-ified!" God reassured him.

The issue is never, "Are you qualified?" The issue is always, "Are you called?"

Have you ever tried out for a team? It can be pretty scary. You worry that you will be the only one who doesn't make the cut. What if you mess up? What if you embarrass yourself?

When you pray, no matter what you pray about, God will reassure you. With each circle of prayer, you will be reminded of God's power and presence. Sometimes the power of prayer is the power to carry on. It doesn't always change your circumstances, but it gives you the strength to walk through them.

What is God calling you to? Will your answer start with "Uhhh, . . . ?" Or will it start with prayer?

Lord, reassure me. Help me step out in faith.

Prayers I'm Circling

....

....

....

....

....

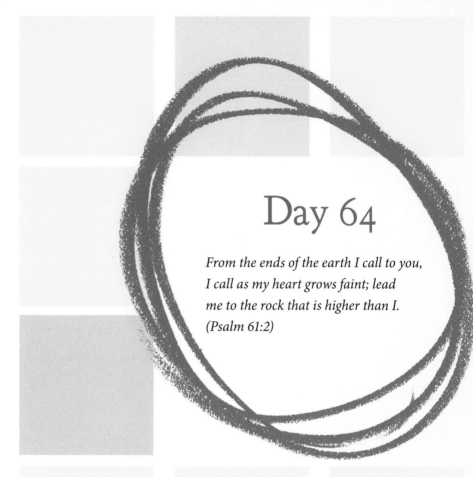

Day 64

From the ends of the earth I call to you,
I call as my heart grows faint; lead
me to the rock that is higher than I.
(Psalm 61:2)

It's normal to be anxious about things like tests, doctor's visits, or bullies at school. Maybe you're nervous about the big game, or even about simply making the team. Even when things seem like easy street to others, you may feel really uneasy on the inside. What do you do when your anxiety feels like it's taking over?

David, in the Bible, knew his share of trouble during his life in pastures and palaces. He faced lions and giants, battle and betrayal, sin and guilt. That's a lot to handle. His anxiety and worry kept him up at night. He even wrote about it. In Psalm 61, he prayed that God would take him to the sheltering rock. David wasn't talking about an actual rock—he was talking about God, strong like a rock, who was over him in heaven, protecting him from all of his fear.

God wants to be your rock too. Next time you feel anxious or scared, find a quiet place, close your eyes, and take a deep breath. Imagine yourself sitting inside the cave of a strong rock where no outside storm can hurt you. Invite Jesus your Savior to sit with you.

I want to build a foundation of faith on your solid Word. Thank you that you are with me, and I don't have to figure it out on my own. Just knowing that makes me feel better.

Prayers I'm Circling

....

....

....

....

....

....

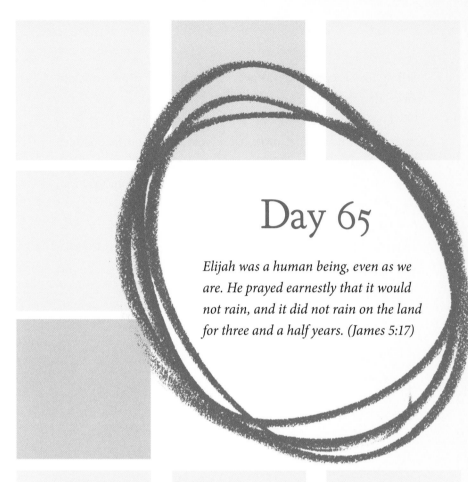

Day 65

Elijah was a human being, even as we are. He prayed earnestly that it would not rain, and it did not rain on the land for three and a half years. (James 5:17)

The prophet Elijah served the Lord, the God of Israel. This was not good news for wicked King Ahab. Elijah humiliated and killed the king's false prophets (450 in all), and he announced a drought that would devastate the wayward nation. Every time Elijah showed up, evil Ahab put his head in his hands.

When the Lord promised Elijah that the long drought would end, the prophet circled the promise with tireless prayer. He climbed to the top of Mount Carmel, bowed his head between his knees, and prayed for rain. Six times he told his servant to look toward the sea, but there was no sign of rain.

Isn't this when most of us would stand up and give up? We

stop praying because we can't see any difference. We look at our circumstances and get discouraged that "nothing is happening." But Elijah remembered the promise, and he prayed some more. When he sent his servant out for the seventh time, a small cloud was rising from the sea. So Elijah said, "Go and tell Ahab, 'Hitch up your chariot and go down before the rain stops you'" (1 Kings 18:44). As the clouds grew thicker and darker, Elijah tucked his cloak into his belt and ran to Jezreel before the king arrived. Wicked King Ahab could never win against the servant of the Lord.

Lord, I'm moved and inspired by Elijah's prayer. I want to be as dedicated to you as Elijah was.

Prayers I'm Circling

....

....

....

....

....

....

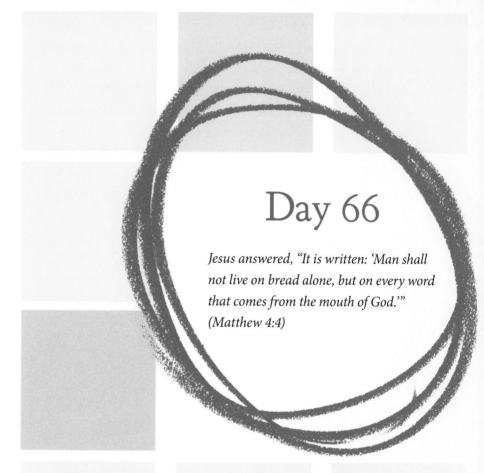

Day 66

Jesus answered, "It is written: 'Man shall not live on bread alone, but on every word that comes from the mouth of God.'"
(Matthew 4:4)

You want a map to spiritual gold? A key to hidden treasure? Open your Bible. Jesus said, "Blessed rather are those who hear the word of God and obey it" (Luke 11:28). The word was inspired by God himself. Disciples wrote it down with ink, but God was the author. He decided what words, stories, and history would bless people around the world for hundreds of years.

While God's Word is holy, there's nothing holy about paper and ink. There's nothing sacred about a leather cover or gold lettering. So feel free to put pen to paper. This is not a library book! It doesn't have to stay clean and tidy. Get a whole set of pens (all the colors of the rainbow) and make your Bible your own as you discover God's Word. Circle his promises so you won't lose them. Underline what inspires you. Star, arrow, asterisk, and highlight everything that stands out to you.

The Bible wasn't meant to just be read through. The Bible was meant to be prayed through. As you read, circle away. And as you circle, pray away. The Bible is a promise book and a prayer book. Reading is the way you get through the Bible. Prayer is the way you get the Bible through you.

Thank you, God, for the Bible, which is priceless to me.

Prayers I'm Circling

....

....

....

....

....

....

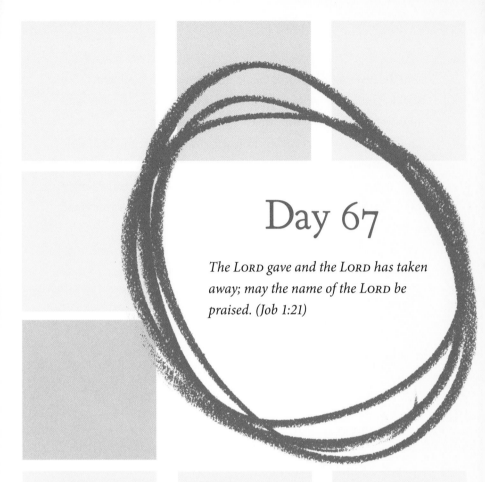

Day 67

The LORD gave and the LORD has taken away; may the name of the LORD be praised. (Job 1:21)

Have you ever thought that a sport was *your life*? Maybe you're never without a ball, or you're always playing and practicing. Maybe you are the best in your school, and better yet, you play for God. That is, you mostly want to win so you can give God glory. You want to be a good sport and give God credit and praise. How would you feel, then, if you badly injured your knee and had to sit out for months?

Maybe you would be angry at first. "God, I was playing for you," you might cry. "How could you let this happen?" You might pray and beg God to heal your knee. After all, you know he could do it, but he might choose not to. How would you respond?

Some of the hardest moments in life are when you've prayed, but the answer is no and you don't know why. And you may never know why, but that is the test of trust. Do you trust that God is *for you* even when he doesn't give you what you asked for? Do you trust that he has reasons beyond your reason? Do you trust that his plan is better than yours?

Our heavenly Father is far too wise and loves us far too much to give us everything we ask for. Someday we'll thank God for every answer to prayer, even the "no." Our frustration will turn to celebration if we keep praying through. I've learned a valuable lesson about unanswered prayer: sometimes God gets in the way to show us the way.

Help me to be faithful even in my disappointments, Lord. I know you love me even when I don't understand.

Prayers I'm Circling

....

....

....

....

....

....

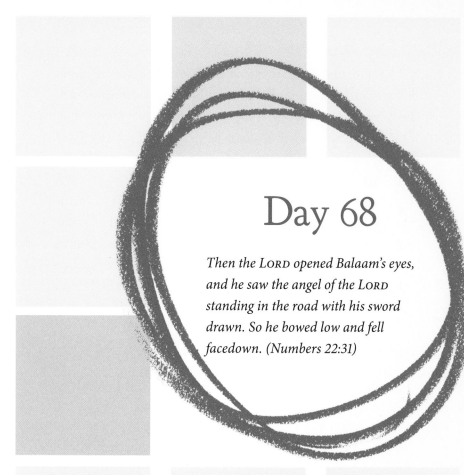

Day 68

*Then the LORD opened Balaam's eyes,
and he saw the angel of the LORD
standing in the road with his sword
drawn. So he bowed low and fell
facedown. (Numbers 22:31)*

One of the wackiest miracles in the Bible involves a talking donkey. In this story, a prophet named Balaam ignored God's plan and went his own way.

Along his journey, an angel stood in the way to block the prophet's progress. Balaam's donkey refused to pass an angel holding a sword. But Balaam didn't see the angel—probably because he wasn't looking. He beat the donkey to keep it moving. The third time this happened, God opened the donkey's mouth. "What have I done to you to make you beat me three times?" it asked.

"You have made a fool of me!" Balaam responded (to a donkey!).

Furious and upset, Balaam was not thinking straight until he saw the angel. "I have come here to oppose you because your path is a reckless one before me," the angel of the LORD said. "The donkey saw me and turned away from me these three times. If it had not turned away, I would certainly have killed you by now, but I would have spared it" (Numbers 22:32–33). The donkey saved the prophet's life!

The real miracle isn't the talking donkey. The real miracle is a God who loves us enough to get in the way when we're going the wrong way. Don't refuse to hear from him. Go to God in prayer so your eyes and ears will be tuned to him.

Lord, help me pay attention to you. I want to go your way, even if it's not a shortcut.

Prayers I'm Circling

....

....

....

....

....

....

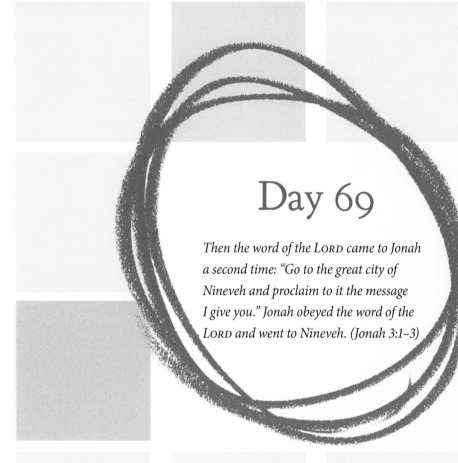

Day 69

Then the word of the LORD came to Jonah a second time: "Go to the great city of Nineveh and proclaim to it the message I give you." Jonah obeyed the word of the LORD and went to Nineveh. (Jonah 3:1–3)

Balaam isn't the only one who overlooked God's directions to stubbornly go his own way. He wasn't the only one who ignored all the chances to turn around. And he wasn't the only one who threw a fit when he couldn't get to where he wanted to go. Most people refuse to go the long way when there's a shortcut!

What if you noticed a chance to cheat on a spelling test? From your desk, you have a clear view of the teacher's answer key. This is great news for you because the spelling words were hard this week and you forgot to study! Now, there's a way to get a good grade. You're ignoring school rules, not to mention God's rules, but maybe the answer key was a sign that God understood that you would do it just this once.

Then, your desk buddy moves his chair a little and now his head is blocking your view of the answers! *Scoot over!* you think to yourself. *He's going to ruin my A+!* The more you think about it, the more annoyed you get.

Just like Balaam and Jonah, you want to go your own way. And God loves you enough to get in the way. Maybe you start thinking better of your sneaky plan. Maybe you find a way to go through with it but get caught cheating—and will never make that mistake again. The point is, listen to God—listen to what the Bible says, listen to the rules and signs that are pointing you in the right direction. Don't wait to hear from a talking donkey or a very large fish! Tune in now.

Thank you for your Word, which shows me where to go. May I have the wisdom to follow it.

Prayers I'm Circling

....

....

....

....

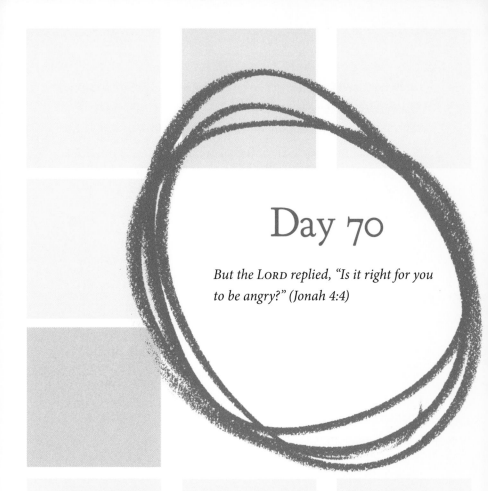

Day 70

But the Lord replied, "Is it right for you to be angry?" (Jonah 4:4)

Jonah had an anger management problem. He couldn't control his temper. Sometimes he was so mad, he couldn't see straight and took matters into his own hands. Sometimes he complained that he was so mad he wanted to die. Sometimes he madly protested that God was too good for wicked people.

Despite this, the Lord and Jonah had a very close relationship. Jonah prayed and confessed openly, and the Lord responded gently. Two times in nine verses, the Lord asked patiently, "Is it right for you to be angry?" And at least two times the Lord saved Jonah with a miracle—once with a fish and once with a plant.

Jonah's anger isn't something to copy. But his openness with God is. Jonah knew that God could handle his honesty, and God can handle yours too. You don't have to fold your hands quietly in your lap and choose your words carefully for God to listen. You don't have to grit your teeth and pretend to smile. If you're angry, upset, or frustrated, admit it to God. God wants your honesty and openness.

Lord, when I feel downright mad and upset, I'm glad you accept me the way I am. I'm glad I can come to you to help me deal with it.

Prayers I'm Circling

....

....

....

....

....

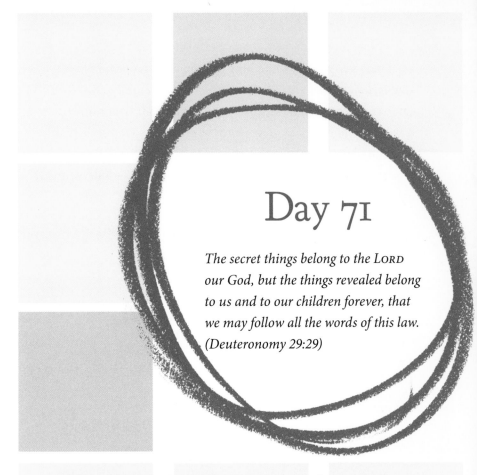

Day 71

The secret things belong to the Lord our God, but the things revealed belong to us and to our children forever, that we may follow all the words of this law. (Deuteronomy 29:29)

The Bible is packed with adventure and advice, history and mystery. We can learn from heroes who have stumbled, from kings who made excellent and terrible choices, and from a loving God who rules over it all. Everything in the Bible is for us to discover, ponder, and pray over.

But there are still countless secrets that only God knows, mysteries that only God understands, questions that only God can answer. Just like your dad carries your suitcase if it is too heavy for you right now, God carries knowledge that is too heavy for his children. While he carries on, we circle verses, like Deuteronomy 29:29, and keep following him.

For example, you might wonder why your uncle is still sick with cancer when you prayed for healing. You might wonder why there was a car accident when you prayed for safety. It's important to dwell on all that you *do* know instead of all that you don't. God is good: 2 Samuel 7:28 tells us, "Sovereign LORD, you are God! Your covenant is trustworthy, and you have promised these good things to your servant." He is with us: Psalm 23:4 says, "Even though I walk through the darkest valley, I will fear no evil, for you are with me." He comforts his children: the writer of Psalm 119:76 proclaimed, "May your unfailing love be my comfort, according to your promise to your servant."

God's Word is full of truth for unexplainable questions. Trust in him.

Lord, thank you for the Bible. I want to know and pray your Word so I can trust you completely.

Prayers I'm Circling

....

....

....

....

....

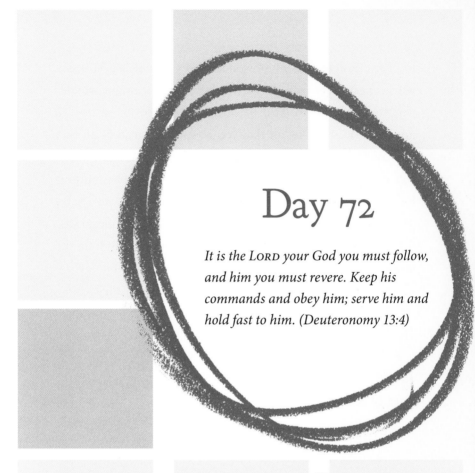

Day 72

It is the LORD your God you must follow, and him you must revere. Keep his commands and obey him; serve him and hold fast to him. (Deuteronomy 13:4)

Remember the game "Follow the Leader"? The person in front does something that the followers have to do too, no matter how silly or crazy? If the leader tiptoes down the street with a cup of water on his head, then his friends are dripping right behind him. If the leader spins down the stairs like a prima ballerina, then their friends prima ballerina right behind. There is pride in being a good follower. But the one in the lead determines the way.

Maybe you haven't played this game for a while . . . or so you think. Have you ever followed the funniest guy in class, even if he's disrespecting the teacher? Maybe it's tempting to follow the most popular girl, even if she's making fun of someone else.

You don't need to play that game. Instead of following the crowd, pick a great leader. After all, if your leader isn't worth following, you might as well sit down. Doing a great job of following someone who is a likable leader isn't awesome if you're headed off a cliff,

The best leader is God. He is worth following. He sees the whole world and knows exactly how everything works. He gives us directions for a reason—to keep us safe and help us live well. So pick up your Bible, and pray where to follow.

Lord, I choose to follow you. Make me strong enough and wise enough to follow you even when my friends are choosing a different way.

Prayers I'm Circling

....

....

....

....

....

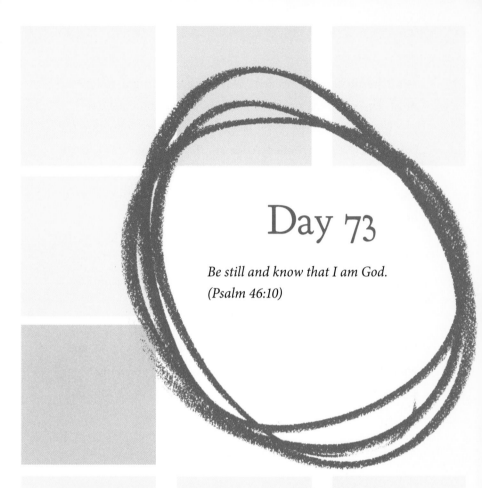

Day 73

Be still and know that I am God.
(Psalm 46:10)

Climbing into a school bus can feel like climbing into a spaceship. Three large steps are the difference between Planet Earth and Alien World. You might see it as an adventure. Or you might find it terrifying.

The Israelites may have seen their exit from Egypt as an adventure. But not long into their journey, it became terrifying. Running from the Egyptians, they had gone as far as they could. The next three large steps would be right into the Red Sea. "Moses answered the people, 'Do not be afraid. Stand firm and you will see the deliverance the LORD will bring you today . . .

The LORD will fight for you; you need only to be still'" (Exodus 14:13–14).

The Israelites stood firm, prayed, and depended on God. He opened up the sea, and the Israelites escaped across dry land. The verse doesn't say, "Do nothing." It doesn't say, "Fight for yourself." Instead, Moses tells them to trust that God will do what he says he will do. He will save his children.

You can do the same thing as you take your seat on the school bus. Be still and know that *he* is God. Stand firm and pray. The rest is in God's hands, and he will see you through.

I trust in you, the God who rescued the Israelites. Thank you for saving your children.

Prayers I'm Circling

....

....

....

....

....

....

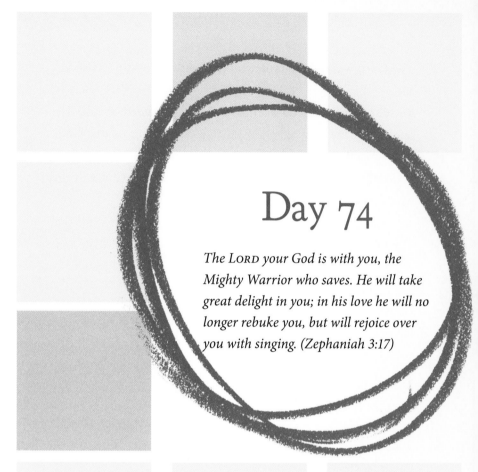

Day 74

The LORD your God is with you, the Mighty Warrior who saves. He will take great delight in you; in his love he will no longer rebuke you, but will rejoice over you with singing. (Zephaniah 3:17)

"I'm doing this for your own good." Have you ever heard someone say this? It usually means the pain you feel now will be a good lesson for you in the long run. The doctor is giving you shots . . . for your own good. Your dad is punishing you . . . for your own good. Your mom is taking away TV . . . for your own good. It may be true, and they may say it as comfort, but it hardly feels like it. It feels more like they're saying, "Brace yourself. Maybe you'll feel better later, maybe you won't." Tough love feels more like "tough" than "love."

Sometimes our worry is that God is all "tough love." We suspect that in order to shape us and make us pure, he's willing to rain down fire . . . for our own good. This false belief colors our view of our heavenly Father, and we shy away from a relationship with the Lord. Basically, we doubt that God is really for us.

Open your Bible and circle Zephaniah 3:17. Take this truth to heart. Memorize it, so that when you're worried or doubting God's love for you, you can say it out loud and never forget.

Lord, it's easy to forget how much you love me. Thank you for your Word, because it reminds me of the unchanging truth.

Prayers I'm Circling

....

....

....

....

....

....

Day 75

Now when Daniel learned that the decree had been published, he went home to his upstairs room where the windows opened toward Jerusalem. Three times a day he got down on his knees and prayed, giving thanks to his God, just as he had done before. (Daniel 6:10)

Daniel didn't start praying when he stepped into the lions' den. He had been praying faithfully his entire life. Three times a day, he stopped what he was doing, dropped to his knees, and became very focused on prayer. He prayed whether he was sick or healthy. He prayed when he faced an ordinary day and when he needed a miracle. He prayed when it was expected and he prayed when it was outlawed by the king. The only thing this superhero of prayer didn't do was wear a cape.

Daniel knew some of his prayers wouldn't be answered in his lifetime. But he knew they would be answered. He prayed toward Jerusalem, a city he knew he would never see again. But he knew prayer was changing him and the people around him. Which is why he stayed faithful in the process.

Praying every day can feel like a long and boring process. Some days you won't want to pray for your family or your day or your problems or your sin. It will feel easier to skip it or turn on the TV and forget about it. But you won't be stronger, wiser, or kinder for it. Be faithful in the process. Your holy Father is waiting for you.

Lord, I know it's important I pray every day. Give me fire and faithfulness for you, because I know you're listening.

Prayers I'm Circling

....

....

....

....

....

....

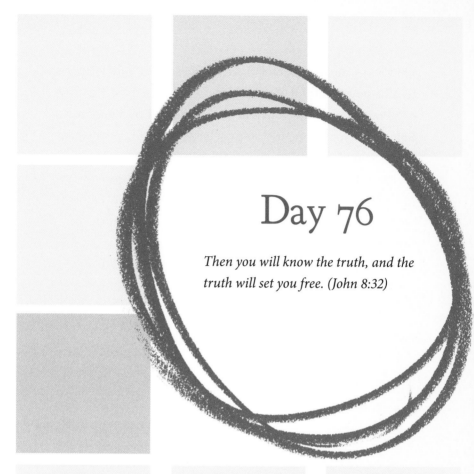

Day 76

Then you will know the truth, and the truth will set you free. (John 8:32)

Have you ever tried on someone else's glasses? Even though it helps them see clearly, it's probably the opposite for you. It changes what you see. Maybe things look a little fuzzy. Maybe everything is a blur. Even when you focus on just one thing, it changes what you see. Take the glasses off, you see one thing. Put the glasses on, the same thing looks completely different. When you can't see clearly, it means you've lost your perspective.

You don't need glasses to change your perspective. Your attitude or point of view can change even when nothing else does. When something bad happens, it's easy to let it ruin your day. Your day hasn't changed, but the way you see it has. Your teacher might correct you in front of the entire class. Or your brother might insult you. Even if the rest of your day is great, your brain might only remember that negative comment. On the other hand, something that you thought was all bad might turn out for the good. A bad grade will remind you to study more. Or a bad move will mean you know better next time. Or a bad decision will give you wisdom to make a better one later.

God's Word has a way of helping you see clearly again. Check out what God has to say about who you are. When you see that he made you uniquely and loves you completely, it's like getting the right perspective. Whatever happens in your day, you can always come back to the truth. Don't settle for blurry vision. Let the truth help you see clearly.

God, help me see things clearly by reading your Word. Help me to believe what the Bible says instead of what other people say.

Prayers I'm Circling

....

....

....

....

....

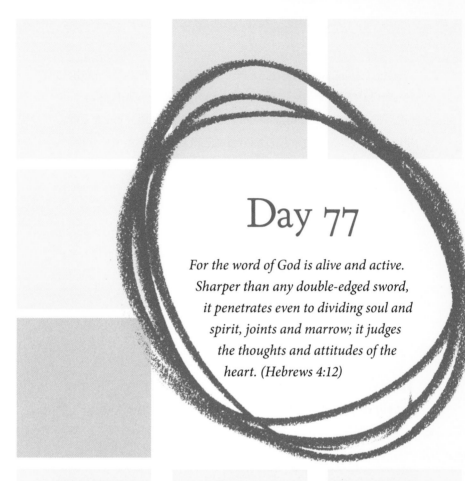

Day 77

*For the word of God is alive and active.
Sharper than any double-edged sword,
it penetrates even to dividing soul and
spirit, joints and marrow; it judges
the thoughts and attitudes of the
heart. (Hebrews 4:12)*

If you were trapped on a desert island and could have three things, what would they be? Maybe a big knife (because it could help get food). Maybe some duct tape (because duct tape fixes everything). Definitely a Bible . . . because Jesus himself was in the desert when he told Satan the truth. "It is written: 'Man shall not live on bread alone, but on every word that comes from the mouth of God'" (Matthew 4:4).

It's good to take care of your body—to make healthy decisions so you can grow strong and feel good. Jesus reminds you to take care of your mind, soul, and spirit too. How? Dive into the Word of God. Take a daily dip into its truth, wisdom, encouragement, and hope. Backed by the power of God himself, the Bible is a lifeline—a direct line to the living God!

On a desert island or in your room, don't forget your Bible! Our most powerful prayers are linked to the promises of God. Write those promises down in this book or in your journal. Bind them to your mind through memorization. Store them in your heart through prayer.

Your Word is powerful, Lord. I want to dive in, pray, and get stronger every day.

Prayers I'm Circling

....

....

....

....

....

....

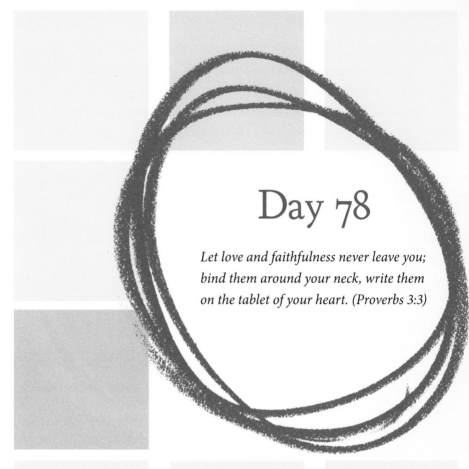

Day 78

Let love and faithfulness never leave you;
bind them around your neck, write them
on the tablet of your heart. (Proverbs 3:3)

A great key to drawing a circle in prayer is to circle God's Word and commit it to memory. If you dwell on it in your mind, it will enter your heart. If it's in your heart, it will affect your faith, your peace, and your actions.

If you struggle with fear, Isaiah 41:10 might comfort you ("So do not fear, for I am with you; do not be dismayed, for I am your God. I will strengthen you and help you; I will uphold you with my righteous right hand.") Then when worry keeps you up at night, you can recite that verse out loud without taking your head off your pillow. If you struggle with doubt, try circling John 16:33 ("I have told you these things, so that in me you may have peace. In this world you will have trouble. But take heart! I have overcome the world.") Then when discouragement creeps up on you, you can use the verse word-for-word to beat it back.

Start small. When you go through the Bible, simply circle verses that are meaningful to you. Then write them down . . . a lot. Write them in your prayer journal with starbursts and swirls. Write them on cards and stick them to the TV. Write them on a postcard to Gramma. Write it with your finger on a steamy mirror after you take a shower. It won't be long until they're written on the tablet of your heart and will never be erased.

Lord, your Word encourages me in all kinds of ways. I can see how memorizing verses will grow my faith in you.

Prayers I'm Circling

....

....

....

....

....

....

Day 79

One day Jesus was praying in a certain place. When he finished, one of his disciples said to him, "Lord, teach us to pray, just as John taught his disciples."
(Luke 11:1)

What kind of art is your favorite? Music? Paintings? Poetry? Ballet? While they all require discipline to create unique beauty, they couldn't be more different. Consider the variety in music alone. Instruments can use strings or keys or mallets or metal or wood to make different music. Rearrange the same notes in different ways and get different music: rock, blues, Motown, pop, opera. It's all music. It's all art. It's all different.

Just like there's no *right* way to make music, there is no *right* way to pray. Music may or may not include words—just like with prayer. Music may require different positions to play—just like with prayer. Music communicates different feelings—just like with prayer.

Try on some of these postures to see which ones feel right for you. You can kneel in humility, stand in praise, sit in reverence, or lay facedown in dependence. Maybe you pray quietly and respectfully in church. Maybe you pray out loud at home so your ears and brain can hear. You can open your eyes for nature's inspiration. You can close your eyes for focus.

Here's an idea you can try: Begin with your hands facing down to symbolize the things we need to let go—our sins, our fears, our control. Then turn your hands over so they are facing up to receive what God wants to give—joy, peace, grace. We receive God's blessings with open hands and open hearts. A sincere heart pleases God no matter what kind of art it's wrapped up in.

It makes me happy, Lord, that you enjoy variety.

Prayers I'm Circling

....

....

....

....

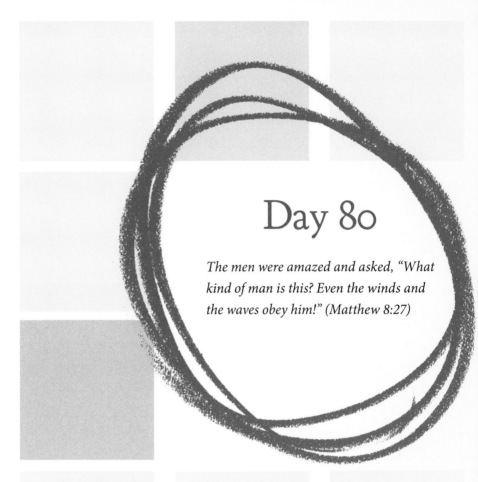

Day 80

The men were amazed and asked, "What kind of man is this? Even the winds and the waves obey him!" (Matthew 8:27)

Matthew 8 shares a story of Jesus and his disciples in a boat on the sea. A storm kicks up, and even the expert fishermen start to fret. The wind grows stronger and the waves grow bigger. While the disciples bail water, Jesus sleeps. Finally, tired and scared, they cry out, "Lord, save us! We're going to drown!"

The disciples had been facing the storm on their own, trying to gut it out and get through it. They struggled with their fear and distress without talking to Jesus. Only when they were desperate did they call out to their Savior. Jesus looked at the faces of his poor disciples and said, "Aww, you guys are so afraid. Why?

I'm right here." He got up, rebuked the winds and the waves, and it became completely calm.

In the middle of a storm, we think we can handle everything on our own. We can handle the anxiety of arguing parents or the stress of school. It doesn't mean we aren't following Jesus, we just think we can grit our teeth, grin, and bear it. Pretty soon the tension becomes so much, we cry out, "Lord, save us!" The thing is, Jesus never expects us to go it alone. If you're worried or anxious, if you have trouble on the outside or on the inside, call out to Jesus now. Tell him your fears, and he will calm the storm in you before it rages out of control. Remember, even the storms obey him.

God, I'm so relieved to be able to call on you for everything. Who else could calm my fears and stress like you?

Prayers I'm Circling

....

....

....

....

....

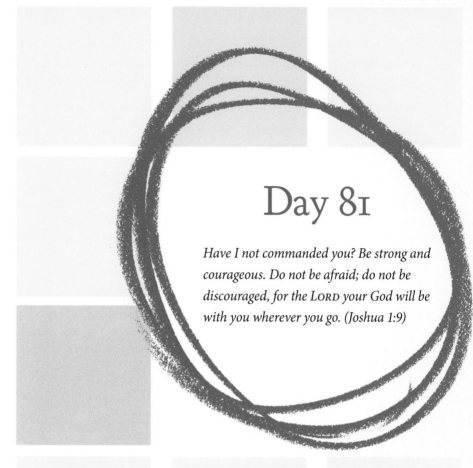

Day 81

Have I not commanded you? Be strong and courageous. Do not be afraid; do not be discouraged, for the LORD your God will be with you wherever you go. (Joshua 1:9)

What dreams keep you awake at night? Maybe you can picture your hopes and goals, but you just can't bring yourself to go after them. Do you want to try out for the lead role in a play? Do you want to talk to a new person at school? Maybe you want to run for class president?

God told his people to be courageous, and his message isn't any different today. He says to go after your dreams. He says not to be afraid. Being courageous doesn't mean your heart won't beat out of your chest. Courage isn't about not having fear. It's about moving forward even when you do have fear. Courage is about whispering prayer and taking one small step in faith. One step toward your dream . . . and then another step after that.

God may not melt away your fear, but he will give you courage to keep moving toward your dream. In turn, your courage and your faith will grow, and your steps will become more sure. The circle around a dream starts with prayer . . . then courage . . . then faith . . . then action. When you come full circle, go again.

Lord, sometimes I let my fear decide what I should do instead of my faith. But I know you can make me brave. I'm happy to ask you for strength and courage.

Prayers I'm Circling

....

....

....

....

....

....

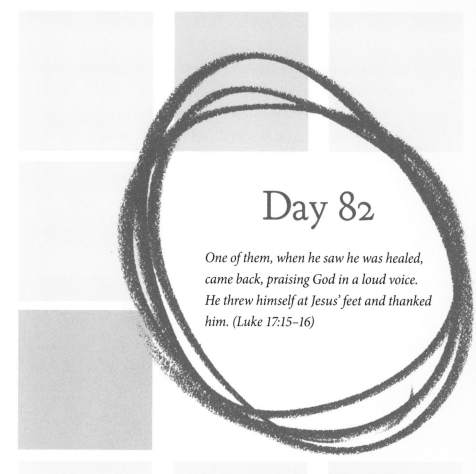

Day 82

One of them, when he saw he was healed, came back, praising God in a loud voice. He threw himself at Jesus' feet and thanked him. (Luke 17:15–16)

Do you remember to say thank you? Do you thank all the people who do "thankless" tasks? Do you thank your friend who bought you a birthday T-shirt even if it was too small? Do you thank your mom for dinner, even though she makes it every night? Do you thank your teacher for the Christmas party she put together?

On the other hand, have you ever done something nice for someone, and they didn't even notice? Maybe you took out the trash and no one said a word. It probably made you a little discouraged. Jesus knows how you feel. He once healed ten people from a terrible disease in one day. Only one of those people came back to thank him! They were all grateful to be healed but forgot to thank the healer. They received a gift but forgot all about the gift-giver.

Sometimes when good things happen, it's easy to get forget to thank God. But prayer isn't just about asking for things or sharing our lives with Jesus. It's also about thanking God. There is so much to be grateful for! God's love, mercy, and grace might top your list. Start circling those things in prayer. You'll find it easier to remember to say thank you.

Lord, sometimes I do forget to thank you, so I thank you now for who you are and for how you love me. Help me to remember every day.

Prayers I'm Circling

....

....

....

....

....

....

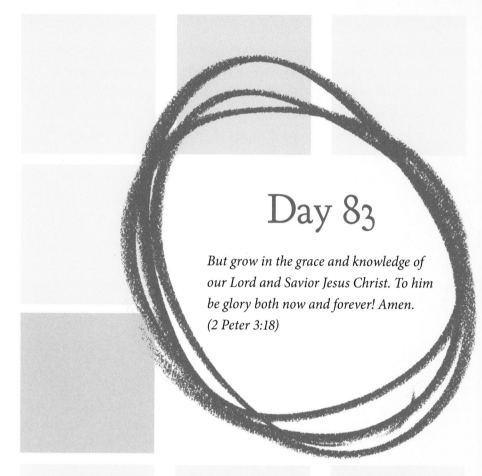

Day 83

But grow in the grace and knowledge of our Lord and Savior Jesus Christ. To him be glory both now and forever! Amen. (2 Peter 3:18)

Now that you are older and in school, it's probably hard to believe you were ever a baby. There was a time when rolling over was a big event and crawling got big cheers. Then you took your first baby step. It took a lot of practice to string a few steps together. There were falls and even a few tears before your baby muscles developed. Now you're such an expert walker, you can keep up with your dad.

God wants you to keep growing in your relationship with him too. He doesn't want you to stay like a tiny baby, always wandering your own way or needing an adult to tell you what you need to know about Jesus. As you grow, you stop crawling and falling and start walking alongside him.

The best ingredients for growing? The Bible and prayer. Feed your mind with a steady diet of these things, and you will get stronger and wiser. The more you know, the more you grow! What verses are you memorizing? Are you praying every day? You probably don't even realize how much you've already grown. The baby Christian is growing up!

When I first met you, Lord, I had no idea how much growing up I would do. I like growing tall, growing up, and growing closer to you.

Prayers I'm Circling

....

....

....

....

....

....

Day 84

[Aaron] took what they handed him and made it into an idol cast in the shape of a calf, fashioning it with a tool. Then they said, "These are your gods, Israel, who brought you up out of Egypt."
(Exodus 32:4)

The Israelites might have been a little confused at first when Aaron made an idol of a cow. After all, it was God they had followed out of Egypt. But when Moses went to the top of a mountain to talk to God, the Israelites began to get restless. In a case of bad judgment, Aaron made a golden calf, like they might have seen when they were back in Egypt.

Prayer isn't powerful or comforting because we do it. Prayer is powerful and comforting because of who we pray to! God is the source of all power and comfort. If they had been praying faithfully, they would not have been distracted by something shiny. If they had been circling the miracles that God was doing right there in the desert, they would not have started worshiping a statue. But their minds and hearts started to wander.

It's easy to get distracted by shiny, new things too, especially when we're not keeping in touch with God. It might be name-brand clothes, it might be a new phone, or it might be anything that comes tied with bow. Idol worship is when we give more worth to an object, a person, or a place than we do to God. He is the only one who deserves our worship.

I confess, Lord, that I get distracted by other things. I know that you are the only thing worthy of worship and praise. Help me stay clear and remember that.

Prayers I'm Circling

....

....

....

....

....

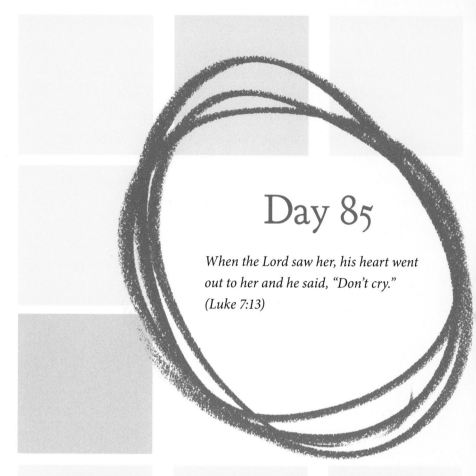

Day 85

When the Lord saw her, his heart went
out to her and he said, "Don't cry."
(Luke 7:13)

Things have changed a lot since the first phone—one that was attached to the wall with a cord. Back in the day, people had books that listed phone numbers. At the same time, a lot of numbers would simply have to be memorized, so if you were at a friend's house, you could use her phone (that was attached to the wall with a cord), and dial in the right number. Now people hardly memorize numbers since you just tap someone's name and the phone dials for you.

Everyone has a number. Every number has a name, every name has a story, and every story matters to God.

I got a letter from a woman whose ID number was on her

jumpsuit. She was in jail and didn't have basic needs like soap. She started circling Philippians 4:19: "And my God will meet all your needs according to the riches of his glory in Christ Jesus." Later that day, she found soap, shampoo, and makeup on her bed. There was also something she hadn't asked for—laundry detergent. From the tone of her letter, you would have thought she had won the lottery!

Behind the number, this woman had a name. And every name has a story that matters to God. What led her to prison matters to him. Her needs matter, her future story matters, and so does her faith!

I praise you, Lord, for never losing track of anyone, never turning your back, never giving up. Thank you for embracing me as your child, whose story matters to you.

Prayers I'm Circling

....

....

....

....

....

....

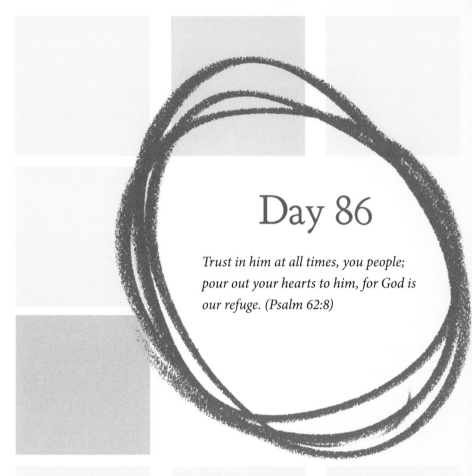

Day 86

Trust in him at all times, you people;
pour out your hearts to him, for God is
our refuge. (Psalm 62:8)

What do you do when you're facing a huge disappointment? Maybe you worked hard on your science project but it didn't turn out the way you wanted. Maybe you've been practicing your basketball shot every single day for months, but the coach hasn't even noticed. Maybe you've had your heart set on the lead in the school play since last year, but didn't get a speaking part.

You aren't the only one to feel upset by setbacks or losses. Your parents have had them too, even as grown-ups. That means you can talk to them, because they know how you feel. You can also talk to God. He understands that your heart feels like it will be bruised forever. Peter broke his own heart when he betrayed Jesus three times. Moses felt disappointment not to see the promised land. David wrote out his prayers of disappointment in the Psalms. For every single one of his children, in every single situation, God knows how to bind up broken hearts.

So don't let disappointment keep you away from the one who can comfort you. If you're experiencing a brand-new setback or if you've been feeling disappointed for days, go to your heavenly Father. Your heart has a safe place in him.

Lord, disappointments are so hard to take, and they feel like they're going to last forever. Please be with me and soothe my hurt.

Prayers I'm Circling

....

....

....

....

....

....

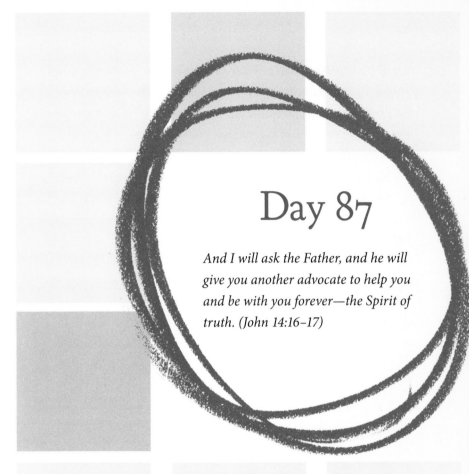

Day 87

And I will ask the Father, and he will give you another advocate to help you and be with you forever—the Spirit of truth. (John 14:16–17)

God has always wanted close relationships with his children. Adam and Eve walked through the garden of Eden talking to God. Moses met with God himself. The Israelites heard the words of God through Moses. Later, Israel's believers (and nonbelievers) heard the words of God through Elijah. God was with them—in a prophet, through an angel, in a dream, on a mountain, in a burning bush, in a pillar of fire, in a still, small voice.

Then God's son himself came to earth to be with the children God loved. After the cross and resurrection, the disciples couldn't believe they were going to be left by themselves. They had gotten used to Jesus' presence and were despondent that he was leaving them. Jesus reassured them. And in Acts, it happened at the Pentecost. The Holy Spirit came down to each individual believer. God is still with us. If Jesus is your Savior, the Holy Spirit is your constant companion, guiding you with wisdom, prompting you with whispers, keeping you safe with a conscience. He is actually praying for you.

So without prophets or Jesus on earth, how do we know where to get God's advice when we need it? Start with prayer. Read the Word. Listen other believers. Pay attention to the Holy Spirit himself.

God made sure that you are never alone. He has spoken to his children through miracles, through prophets, through Jesus, through the Holy Spirit, through the Bible, through other believers, You, my friend, are never alone. God with us (Immanuel) is God is with *you*.

Dear God, you're my advice giver, my counselor, my constant companion. Thank you for giving me all these ways to feel confident in your presence.

Prayers I'm Circling

....

....

....

....

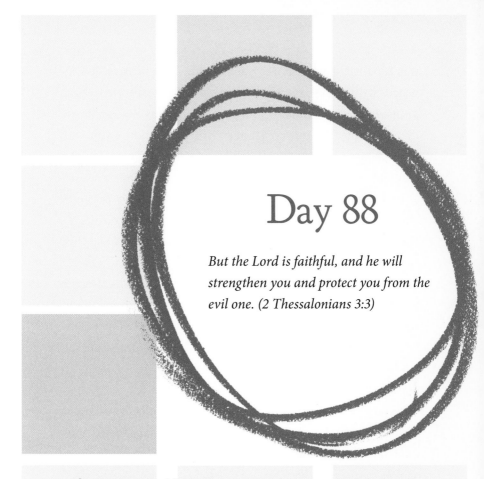

Day 88

But the Lord is faithful, and he will strengthen you and protect you from the evil one. (2 Thessalonians 3:3)

A "sitting duck" is a person with no protection against danger. Even a running duck would be in trouble, but a sitting duck has no chance. If you're running a football without a defensive line, you're a sitting duck about to be clobbered. If you're swinging a stick at a beehive in the middle of nowhere? Quack, quack. If you hang out with the kids in school who like to cause trouble (even if you don't), you will likely get swept up like quackers.

When pursued by danger, do you act like a sitting duck, or do you run for shelter? The Lord has been compared to a strong tower. The righteous run into it and they are safe. This happens first in prayer. Maybe you pray, "Lord, I'm glad I got invited to this slumber party, but I don't want to watch this bad movie they're turning on. Show me what to do." In prayer, you've reminded yourself that you're not alone like a sitting duck. You've got the Holy Spirit guiding you. Maybe he'll suggest you go to bed early, play a game with someone in the other room, call your mom, or roll over and recite some Scripture.

God says that when hard times come, he wants to be your safe place. If you are afraid or worried or stuck, go to him and he'll take care of you. He's faithful—he'll never leave you alone and never fail. Don't waddle around wondering what to do, just hoping you don't get clobbered. Call out to Jesus. He's already there. All you have to do is ask for his help.

Dear God, thank you for keeping me safe. I trust you and love you for being with me.

Prayers I'm Circling

....

....

....

....

....

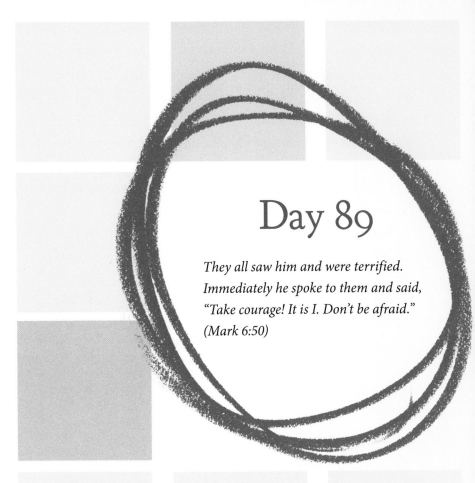

Day 89

They all saw him and were terrified.
Immediately he spoke to them and said,
"Take courage! It is I. Don't be afraid."
(Mark 6:50)

The disciples were in the middle of a storm. They were stuck on the water in the dark of the night, trying to take care of their boat . . . and themselves. Scared and tired, they struggled with the nets, with the waves, with their fear. Then, as if things weren't tense enough, they saw something on the water. What was it? Some fog? No. A . . . ghost?

But it wasn't a ghost at all! It was Jesus. When they didn't know what to do, Jesus came to them, walking on water. In the middle of nowhere, a miracle was arriving. In the middle of their fear and fatigue, Jesus was coming to meet them. In the middle of a storm, they were surprised to find him there.

The disciples aren't the only ones who got tired and afraid. They aren't the only ones who battled a storm in the sky, waves on the sea, and trouble in their hearts. Whatever's worrying you today—sickness, loss of friendships, even frightening TV shows you maybe shouldn't have watched—there is Jesus. Where it seems impossible for him to be, nothing could keep him away. He can calm the sea. He can calm your heart. "Don't be afraid," he says. "It's me. I'm here."

Thank you, Jesus, for being with me when things get scary. I feel better and braver knowing you are here today.

Prayers I'm Circling

....

....

....

....

....

Day 90

And we know that in all things God works for the good of those who love him, who have been called according to his purpose. (Romans 8:28)

Do you know a key ingredient for cookies is salt? Isn't that weird? You wouldn't put salt *on* a cookie, but you always put it *in* one. You also wouldn't lick up a plain handful of salt. But in a cookie, salt is actually very good. In fact, you need the salt to make the cookie delicious.

Salt is like hard times. On their own, they're hard to take, especially in big amounts. Plus, they leave a bad taste in your mouth long after they're over. But Paul reassured God's children. He said that the salt people taste now—their suffering—is part of something better—God' plan. God's whole plan comes together like a gourmet cookie.

Some ingredients in the recipe of your life might not make sense. Why does God allow sadness, frustration, or anger? Why does he include mean people and messy situations in your life? Because he knows the entire recipe. He knows how it's all going to come together for good.

Trust that God is not serving salt as the main course. It's just a small part that makes the rest of your life sweeter. Trust it's coming together under the watchful eye of the Master Chef.

Lord, I know that you're working out something very good, even if I don't understand it right now. Help me to keep praying through. I trust you, and look forward to your plan.

Prayers I'm Circling

....

....

....

....

....

....

Day 91

*Then they said, "Come, let us build
ourselves a city, with a tower that reaches
to the heavens, so that we may make a
name for ourselves; otherwise we will
be scattered over the face of the whole
earth. (Genesis 11:4)*

I love God-sized dreams. But if your dream is for your own fame, know that God might take you in another direction. God knows that fame is hard on a relationship with him, so he doesn't choose life in the spotlight for everyone. It's very hard to be famous and still completely rely on God with all your heart.

Popularity can make it super hard to make godly but unpopular decisions. If you're worried about what others think, it's easier to disregard what God thinks. For example, it's a lot easier to sit with your friends than to sit with the lonely, new kid.

In Genesis 11, God's people had a big dream to build a monument . . . to themselves. Altars were built throughout the

Bible, but they were monuments to God. They remembered and praised what God had done. The Tower of Babel was different, because it was intended to show how great the builders were, not how great the Creator was. The people wanted to make a name for *themselves*. But God didn't share that spotlight. Instead, he confused their languages. Without the ability to communicate, they stopped work on the tower and scattered.

It's okay to pray for your big dreams. But also pray that they would be for God's glory, not your own. Confess if you have doubt about whether the fame is for you or for God. Just going after God's own heart will make sure you're not in it for yourself.

I pray to you as my Lord and Savior. I want to give you the credit you deserve.

Prayers I'm Circling

....

....

....

....

....

....

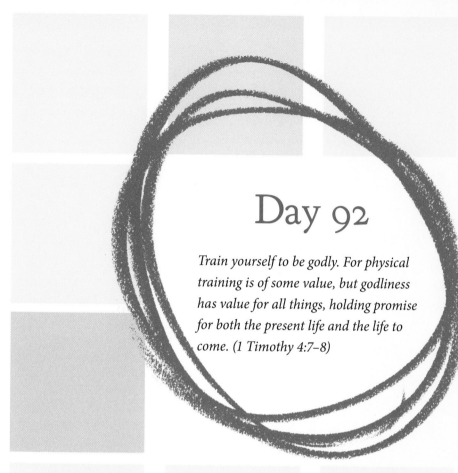

Day 92

Train yourself to be godly. For physical training is of some value, but godliness has value for all things, holding promise for both the present life and the life to come. (1 Timothy 4:7–8)

When you watch the Olympics, it's exciting to see athletes at the top of their game. In front of cheering crowds, they come together for two short weeks to compete at the highest level. What you don't see on TV is the days, months, and years they spend training. Every day, they get up early to practice in quiet places far from cheering crowds. They warm up, sweat through ordinary drills, and polish their skills. They meet with coaches who know how they should train, what they should eat, and how they should think. And they do it every day, whether they feel like it or not. Only then will they be ready to perform their sport so well when the time comes.

In some ways, you're just like an Olympic athlete. You're in training too. Every day, you meet with your coach in heaven who guides you in your discipline. Every ordinary day, you set your sights on him and practice prayer. Do the training, and you will love your neighbor well. Do the training, and you will be a light to your friends and family. Do the training, and you grow closer to God each day.

Reading the Bible and praying are training for strength in godliness. These aren't things meant to show off to cheering crowds, but to honor the Lord. He is cheering you on!

Lord, I want to be more like you. Help me show up to practice my spiritual disciplines every day so that I can know you better.

Prayers I'm Circling

....

....

....

....

....

....

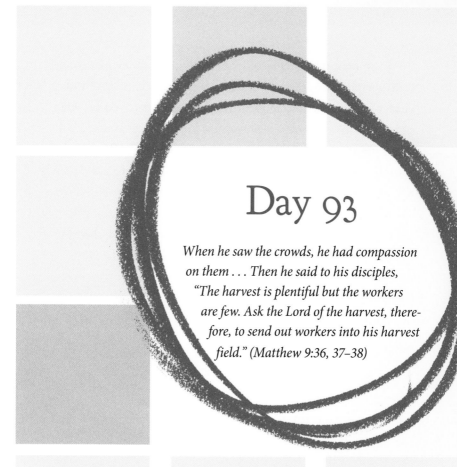

Day 93

When he saw the crowds, he had compassion on them ... Then he said to his disciples, "The harvest is plentiful but the workers are few. Ask the Lord of the harvest, therefore, to send out workers into his harvest field." (Matthew 9:36, 37–38)

Jesus is Lord over all the earth, but not everyone in this wide world knows it. He loves and has compassion for everyone, and he wants every single person to know his good news. So his followers have the important job of introducing others to the Savior.

God *could* send his angels to the sky to announce him like he did when Jesus was born. But he *chooses* to send his children around the world to talk about him. You might be a disciple to your city, showing the love of Jesus to your neighbors. Or you might support missionaries who go farther away to introduce Jesus to places where they have not heard God's message.

Jesus sees every person with love and compassion. Whether they are in your state or across the globe, he says those people are like a crop that's ready for harvest—they're ready to hear about him. They need people to "work the field." You can ask Jesus to send his messengers to work the field near and far, and ask him to help you talk to the people around you. One day you might find out that someone knows Jesus because you yourself prayed!

Lord, I pray for those around the world who don't know you. I pray you'll send workers into the field to help them.

Prayers I'm Circling

....

....

....

....

....

....

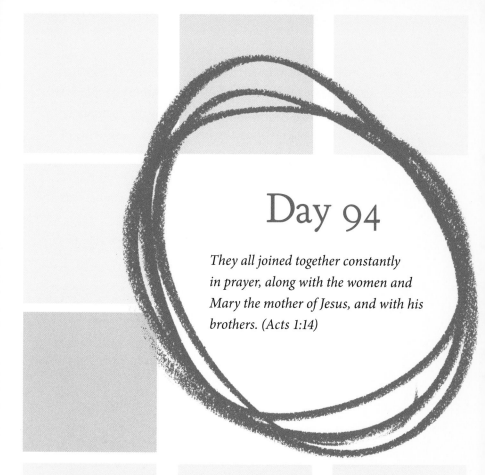

Day 94

They all joined together constantly in prayer, along with the women and Mary the mother of Jesus, and with his brothers. (Acts 1:14)

Prayer can be a private conversation between you and God, but it doesn't have to be. Bring others into your prayer circle to see how prayer changes for you.

If you are in a small group of people, you can form a circle and pray together. That is, one person prays, and when he stops, another person starts to pray out loud. You can also pray like a lot of churches do—a leader prays out loud, while the congregation silently prays along in support. Some people prefer to make a "prayer chain." An example of a prayer chain is if your friend wants prayer for her sick dog, she might call you. You could pray and then call another friend with the same prayer request to pass it on.

Praying with others changes a solo act into a community one. There's nothing more bonding than praying together. When people humbly come before God, it's hard to feel alone. Plus, you see that God can work in big ways.

Jesus prayed to his Father by himself, and he prayed in groups. He prayed with his disciples before he took the cup at the Last Supper, and he prayed by himself before he went to the cross. Prayer is a good thing, whether you go solo or in groups. Try them both and see how God moves in you.

Lord, teach me to pray in all kinds of ways, in all kinds of spaces.

Prayers I'm Circling

....

....

....

....

....

....

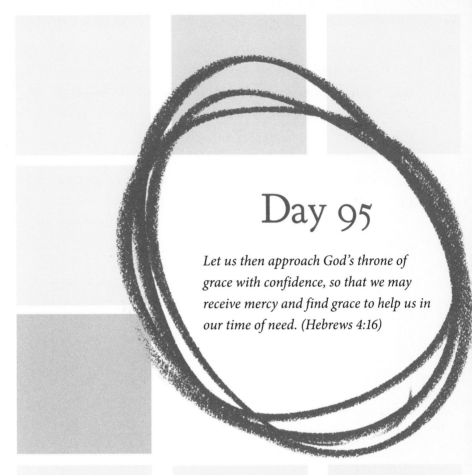

Day 95

Let us then approach God's throne of grace with confidence, so that we may receive mercy and find grace to help us in our time of need. (Hebrews 4:16)

If you could meet any famous person, who would it be? A ball-player maybe, or your favorite singer? If they're really famous, they might not even be able to count their fans. Who knows how many people adore them based on what they see on social media or TV or in a magazine. Unfortunately for fans, it's not an easy process to meet famous people. They have bodyguards and SUVs with black-tinted windows and gated houses and backdoor exits. To get an appointment with them, you must know the right number to the right person who knows the right person who can find time in a very busy schedule.

When you consider how difficult it is to meet with a famous

person, it's even more surprising that you can meet directly with God! He doesn't require an appointment or a dark limousine to keep out onlookers. He's not surrounded by handlers that keep the riffraff out. He's never too busy, or too stressed out, or too important to meet up with you. You don't need to be well-connected or know a secret handshake. You are welcome . . . always . . . just the way you are.

No matter how far you are, you're only one step away from the living God. Come to the throne room with confidence. The King is waiting for you.

Lord, it feels so good to know you want to meet with me. Thank you for making it so easy to come close to you. Thank you for personally welcoming me.

Prayers I'm Circling

....

....

....

....

....

Day 96

*We have this hope as an anchor for
the soul, firm and secure. It enters the
inner sanctuary behind the curtain.
(Hebrews 6:19)*

When Adam and Eve disobeyed God in the garden of Eden, sin entered the world. Sin separates a perfect God from the people he loves.

Before Jesus died on the cross, priests were the bridge that people had to use to get to God. Only the high priest was allowed to enter past a curtain to the inner-most room of the temple called the Holy of Holies. Plus, the priests performed ceremonies and sacrifices for the people. The sacrifices paid for sin until the next sacrifice. Priests played a key role in the relationship between God and his people.

Jesus changed everything. He was the perfect, spotless

sacrifice that fulfilled the law once and for all. *He* is now the bridge between people and God. The curtain that hung in the temple that separated the Holy of Holies was torn in two, so there is no longer a barrier. Because of Jesus, we now have direct access to God.

We no longer have to make sacrifices. Jesus was the ultimate sacrifice. We no longer have to go through a priest to approach God. Jesus is our high priest. Because of Jesus, we have life and hope!

Thank you, Jesus, for your sacrifice that washed away my sin. I would be lost if you didn't rescue me. I'm so glad I can come to you any time and all the time.

Prayers I'm Circling

....

....

....

....

....

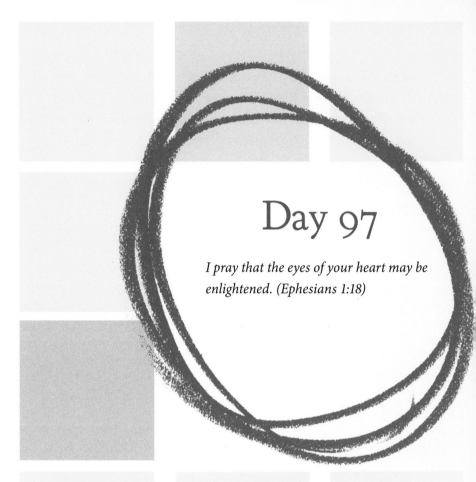

Day 97

I pray that the eyes of your heart may be enlightened. (Ephesians 1:18)

Have you ever been sitting outside when a friend walks up to you? If the sun is behind them, shining in your eyes, you won't be able to make out their face at all. But if you shade your eyes and move a little, you can see who has been standing there all along.

Reading the Bible can feel like looking into the sun and trying to make out what's there. Without the Holy Spirit, it can be hard to see what you're looking at. You might have questions, like why does God allow hard things to happen to good people? Why is it really so important to forgive? Why do some things work out while others don't? God is not trying to confuse you; you need to ask God to help you make sense of these hard questions.

When you know Jesus, you start to see the Bible without the sun in your eyes. The more time you spend reading and praying, the more the Holy Spirit takes the glare out of your eyes, so you can see the real picture. The more you read, the more you see, the more you understand.

Dear God, I want to see the truth. Help me understand your Word. Teach me as I pray.

Prayers I'm Circling

....

....

....

....

....

....

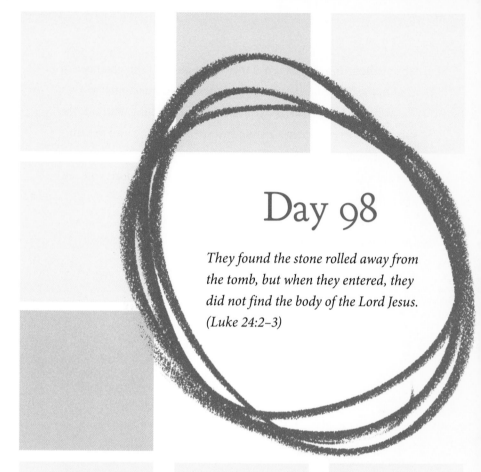

Day 98

They found the stone rolled away from the tomb, but when they entered, they did not find the body of the Lord Jesus. (Luke 24:2–3)

When Jesus died, his followers couldn't believe it. They expected the King of Kings to sit on a throne, not die on a cross. They didn't understand! Three days later, they went to Jesus' tomb. They expected to be blocked by the massive stone that closed the tomb, but it had been moved. When the angel of the Lord appeared to them, they couldn't believe it! Jesus was alive?

God knows it can be hard for us to understand too, but he is with you even when you feel alone. God answers your prayers, even if it's not the way you expected. God has a magnificent rescue plan, even if you can't see it all right now. You may not be able to grasp it all right away. That's okay. Circle it in prayer. Ask God to help you understand. Ask him to help you believe his good news. Ask him to give you faith in his character. He will. Keep circling. God is faithful.

Remember, the stone was rolled away. Jesus is alive and powerful, ready to show you the way.

Lord, sometimes what I feel at the moment and what I know in my head are different. Give me faith to believe your Word even if I don't completely understand.

Prayers I'm Circling

....

....

....

....

....

....

Day 99

The end of a matter is better than its beginning, and patience is better than pride. (Ecclesiastes 7:8)

Toward the end of his life, Honi the circle maker was walking down a dirt road when he saw a man planting a carob tree. Honi stopped. "How long will it take this tree to bear fruit?" he asked.

"Seventy years," the man answered.

Honi looked at the man. "Are you sure you will live another seventy years to eat its fruit?" he asked.

"Perhaps not," the man replied. "However, when I was born into this world, I found many carob trees planted by my father and grandfather. Just as they planted trees for me, I am planting trees for my children and grandchildren. They will be able to eat the fruit of these trees."

Honi realized that praying is planting. Each prayer is like a seed that gets planted in the ground. It disappears for a season, but it eventually bears fruit. Maybe he would taste that fruit. Maybe it would feed future generations after he was gone. But he realized our prayers bear fruit forever.

The fruit of your prayers might blossom by the end of the year, by the time you graduate from school, or by the time your hair grows gray. Your patience along with the plan of the Master Gardener will ensure that the fruit is sweet.

Lord, I want to plant seeds with prayer. Let them grow and bear good fruit.

Prayers I'm Circling

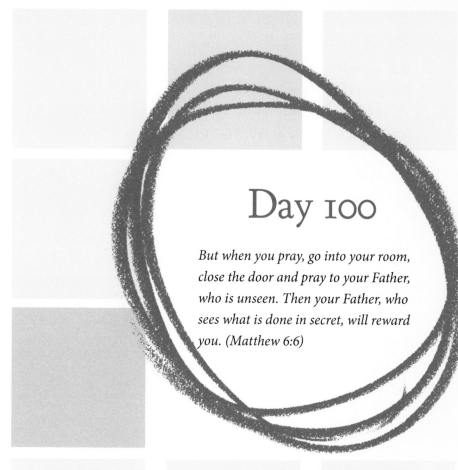

Day 100

But when you pray, go into your room, close the door and pray to your Father, who is unseen. Then your Father, who sees what is done in secret, will reward you. (Matthew 6:6)

If you're not convinced that prayer is for you, consider this: You don't have to be good, smart, grown up, popular, or put together. You don't need a smart phone, a killer bike, a partner, or an adult. You don't need to know any answers, any people, or even any Bible verses. All you have to be is totally, completely, utterly *you*.

Prayer is never out of reach. It's on the bottom shelf. If you're not sure you can reach it, just get on your knees. Don't let what you cannot do keep you from doing what you can. Draw the circle.

All it takes is one person, one prayer. Why not you? It's as simple as drawing your first prayer circle. It might be around a promise or a problem. It might be around a friend or an enemy. It might be around a dream or a miracle. It might even be around *you*. Maybe you need a miracle! Draw the circle.

Prayer is the difference between the best you can do and the best God can do. What God does for us isn't just for us. Just as the blessings, breakthroughs, and miracles in your life are an answer to someone else's prayer, your prayers will bless and impact others. So you do you—and see where God takes you.

I'm so glad you listen to me even though I'm a beginner in prayer. I will keep circling.

Prayers I'm Circling

....

....

....

....

....

....

Mark Batterson is the *New York Times* bestselling author of fifteen books, including *The Circle Maker*, *All In*, *Chase the Lion*, and *Whisper*. He serves as lead pastor of National Community Church in Washington, D.C. One church with eight campuses, NCC also owns and operates Ebenezers Coffeehouse, the Miracle Theatre, and the DC Dream Center. Mark has a doctor of ministry degree from Regent University. He and his wife, Lora, have three children and live on Capitol Hill.